# SpringerBriefs in Applied Sciences and Technology

## Ethical and Legal Issues in Biomedicine and Technology

**Series editor**

Giovanni Boniolo, University of Ferrara, Ferrara, Italy

More information about this series at http://www.springer.com/series/13628

Adriano Fabris

# Ethics of Information and Communication Technologies

Springer

Adriano Fabris
Dip. di Civilta e Forme del Sapere
Pisa
Italy

ISSN 2191-530X ISSN 2191-5318 (electronic)
SpringerBriefs in Applied Sciences and Technology
SpringerBriefs on Ethical and Legal Issues in Biomedicine and Technology
ISBN 978-3-319-75510-6 ISBN 978-3-319-75511-3 (eBook)
https://doi.org/10.1007/978-3-319-75511-3

Library of Congress Control Number: 2018933477



Printed on acid-free paper

This Springer imprint is published by the registered company Springer International Publishing AG part of Springer Nature
The registered company address is: Gewerbestrasse 11, 6330 Cham, Switzerland

# Preface

This book aims to provide an introduction to information and communication technologies from an ethical perspective. This is an introduction that does not want to focus solely on what these technologies are and on how they work. Certainly, some of the insights on this subject will be offered in the book, as it has been written bearing in mind that it is dedicated to a non-specialist audience. But the purpose of the book is different: it wants to clarify what are the correct and good ways for human beings to relate today to information and communication technologies.

This is an ethical task. Ethics is the study of the domains of human life characterised by codified behaviours and habits (which the ancient Greeks called ethos), to analyse how we move and interact with them, to identify the criteria and principles which in these areas allow us to make the best decisions, to clarify what the terms "good" and "bad" in relation to our actions properly mean and to motivate the choice of something good. To elaborate an ethics, therefore, it is necessary to discuss these various problems, to highlight the moral dilemmas that may arise therein and to justify the reason why we define certain behaviours as being good or not.

The environments in which we live in today are characterised by the massive and widespread presence of information and communication technologies. We find ourselves in a constant flow of information, both in the real world and in virtual environments. We live inserted in an ever-expanding global data stream.

The transmission of data, however, is not the only way information and communication work. Technology itself, as it is conceived and produced today, works in turn as data transmission. In other words, if you assume the idea of communication as a means of transmitting data and information, consequently technology itself has a communicative structure as such independently whether it serves to communicate certain content to someone. More importantly, if we are to critically confront ourselves with the age we live in, an ethical in-depth study of this situation is indispensable.

Chapter 1 of this book presents an analysis of the notion of "technology", the way it differs from the traditional notion of "technique" and the forms in which technology works. The chapter then introduces the ways in which today's reflection and ethical practice are understood. It goes from a general study of the principles of acting to the discussion of the most concrete moral problems that arise in certain areas where they are applied; from the definition of a set of behavioural prescriptions, which is provided by professional deontology, to the justification of the wider moral orientation that is implicit in the action of each human being.

Chapter 2 is about how the technological devices we use most widely, even for communicating, affect our behaviour: the computer, the smartphone, the robot (considered as an interactive communication system). In this chapter, we question ourselves on the ways in which we interact with such devices, the problems that arise in this interaction and about the choices we have to make from time to time. These are important issues and choices, as these devices, like a kind of "Keymaster", give access to real or virtual environments of communication in which we live and interact with each and every day.

Finally, Chap. 3 is dedicated to the in-depth analysis of these environments that are made possible by the latest technological developments. These are mostly virtual environments in which flows of information are the background in which we carry out our concrete communicative activity. Therefore, after an analysis of what is commonly called "virtual reality", some ethical issues concerning the Internet of Netsurfers, the Internet of Social Networks and the Internet of Things are presented and discussed.

In brief, the overall aim of this book is to provide a picture of the situation we live in today, in the age of information and communication technologies, the problems that this situation has and the ways in which it is possible to address them from an ethical point of view. More specifically—given that photography provides a fixed image, while technology is developing dynamically and without stopping—what the book intends to present is a series of frames, a few segments from movies, from which one can obtain and analyse the conditions in which we live in, including some trends regarding the future scenarios of communication. Moreover, this reference to cinema is not inappropriate: very often, in the book, issues are exemplified with reference to some famous movies.

Pisa, Italy Adriano Fabris

*The original version of the book was revised:*
*Copyright page text has been updated.*
*The erratum to the book is available at*
*https://doi.org/10.1007/978-3-319-75511-3_4*

# Acknowledgements

This book could not have been written without the help of Leigh-Anne Mazzoncini, for the English revision, and of Andrea Tomasi, for all the engineering terms (both at Pisa University, Italy). Some important suggestions came from Pierre Lévy (University of Ottawa, Canada) and Marcello Vitali Rosati (Canada Research Chair on Digital Textualities, Université de Montréal). To all of them, I give my deepest gratitude. Many thanks, finally, to Luca Valera, Universidad Católica de Chile (Santiago de Chile), who gave me the opportunity to discuss my project with his research group on Applied Ethics.

# Contents

# Chapter 1
# Basic Concepts

**Abstract** To begin with, the first chapter will clarify the difference between "technique" and "technology". Technique is considered the extension of a human action through the use of various kinds of tools. Technology, on the other hand, is considered a technical system, a field where it is possible to develop acts which are largely independent from human actions and where there are devices able to interact with the environment within which they carry out their procedures. The following section develops the distinction between technique and technology by considering the more specific field of information and communication processes and by introducing the world of Information and Communication Technologies (ICTs). The distinction between techniques and technologies of information and communication is exemplified through the history of the tools and devices used over time for writing, printing and reading. It is necessary, however, to distinguish between "information" and "communication". Information is the transmission of data from a sender to a receiver. It mainly consists of mechanical relationships and indeed characterizes the very functioning of some machinery. Communication is the ability to create and share a common space among interlocutors. This is a typically human process. Considering that the topic of this book is the ethics of information and communication technologies, in this first chapter it is also necessary to explain the meaning of the term "ethics" and to describe the main trends present in contemporary ethics. The subject of "applied ethics" and the relation between applied ethics and general ethics are just introduced and discussed here, as much as the difference between the ethical and the deontological approach. In the final section of this chapter, I will lay out another difference concerning our daily experience within the areas of information and communication. It is the difference among the use of specific techniques, the interaction with various technologies and the possibility, that we have more and more today, of living in virtual environments. Considered both from a deontological and ethical point of view, this involves the development of two specific lines of in-depth study on our theme: the study on communication devices and that on communication environments. They will be developed in the second and in the third chapter of this book.

 
A. Fabris, *Ethics of Information and Communication Technologies*,
SpringerBriefs on Ethical and Legal Issues in Biomedicine and Technology,
https://doi.org/10.1007/978-3-319-75511-3_1

**Keywords** Technique · Technology · Information · Communication
Deontology · Ethics · Applied ethics

## 1.1 Technique and Technology

The movie begins when an ape tries to get close to a pool of water to quench his thirst. Other apes stop him from doing this because they consider that water a property of their tribe. Chased away, the ape moves on. He is attracted by the skeleton of a decaying animal lying in the sun. He spots the thigh-bone of the skeleton, grabs it and starts banging it on the ground. The ape then hits the skull of the skeleton, and breaks it. The ape realizes that the bone can be used as a weapon.

After a few sequences our protagonist returns to the waterhole. But this time he is holding the bone that he picked up off the ground. When the tribe's chief approaches the ape to chase him away again, the ape uses the bone to beat the chief. He hits him over and over again, until the opponent can't get up anymore. The other apes runaway. He remains master of the land and has access to the waterhole. In a sign of victory he tosses the bone up in the air and, as it turns in the sky, it becomes a spaceship orbiting in space.

For those who have never seen Stanley Kubrick's *2001: A Space Odyssey*, the movie opens with the scene I have just described. But what does this scene tell us? And what does the ape, the bone and the spaceship have to do with what I would like to express in this chapter on techniques and technologies and what they have in common and how they differ?

The movie, with respect to this subject, can tell us a lot, but it can also mislead us. First of all it tells us what the technique is. The technique is what expands the possibilities of the actions human beings take. The strength of the ape's arm would not have been sufficient enough to have the upper hand over the tribe that wanted to prevent the ape from reaching the water. What was necessary was an extension of the arm, an energy booster, and knowledge on how to use it. The technique enhances human capabilities and allows us to achieve results that, without it, it would be impossible to reach. The technique is a form of practical knowledge (Aristotle 1924, I, 1, 981 a 5–981 b 25) that, by using certain tools already present in nature or built for a certain purpose, can extend the scope of the actions we take.

How does the technique come to be? Firstly, it comes from the awareness of the lack of something and from the consciousness of our own limitations. The ape realizes that he cannot face the other apes on his own. Then, the condition so that a technique can develop is given by the adaptability of the human being, and by the ability to change our behaviour in order to fill that gap, or better so the lack of something. The human being, and before that, our ape, is structurally adaptable (Gehlen 1988). Whereas the giraffe has a long neck to collect the leaves and fruit high up on the tree, the polar bear has a brute force able to break the bones of its prey, humans can extend the reach of their arm and break the bones of an opponent just by using a stick. But can we use a stick only because we can hold it, or can we hold it only because we have a hand that has a thumb. The structure of the hand is not sufficiently specialized enough to achieve only one result (scratching with nails, or smashing with a fist), but it is made in a way so that it can be supplemented by various technical tools.

All of this is not enough to make the technique come to life. We need to look at the world from another prospect, using our sense of imagination. We need to look at things and see in them as something different than what they are. The bone of the ape in *2001: A Space Odyssey* is not simply a bone for him, but *he sees it as a weapon*. The human capacity to imagine the possible uses of something, the scenarios of their possible application, gives us the ability to transform a pure and simple thing into a tool. What is more, this tool fits into a context of broader relations, within which the device serves a purpose that is designed to achieve a goal.

The ape's behavior in Kubrick's movie demonstrates this very well. It does not matter if his imagination, his ability to see beyond the pure and simple, is inspired by an external power—which in the movie is symbolized by a black monolith—or simply by chance. The fact remains that the ape does not see the bone simply as a bone, but also and above all, in this example, he sees it as a weapon. However, the movie also takes on a misleading approach different to what we have discussed. This is evident in the final part of the episode in which the bone, thrown into the air, turns into a spaceship.

It appears in fact from these frames that between the bone as a weapon used by the ape and the spaceship, or better yet, between a simple technical tool and a complex technological machine, there is a complete sense of continuity. The relationship between a bone used for striking and an environment that enables human beings to live and move in space seems to be only one connected to progressive development and a growing complexity of the instruments used. On the other hand, the relationship between technique and technology requires a great shift in the paradigm. This is evident when considering the history of technology (Singer et al. 1957).

We could say in fact that technology is a technical system (Ellul 1964; Jerónimo et al. 2013). This means that in technology many techniques are connected and coordinated among themselves to achieve the same goal. In the history of mankind many examples of these types of instruments have been combined in increasingly complex inventions, which have interacted with the human environment by transforming it. Some examples that we can mention are: the mechanical clock (made of levers, gears, wheels, springs all connected one with the other), the factory according to Taylor's organization (based on the principle of the assembly line in which different machines are coordinated with one another) and, today, the Google Car (the car can follow the road without a driver, reaching the predetermined destination).

All reference to these examples, however, reveals a fundamental aspect of technology which allows to distinguish it further more from the technique, but also to show the historical line of development that leads from technique to technology. The stick requires a hand that can hold it and use it. To work, the mechanical watch needs someone to charge it, but then it works automatically. The factory consists of machines that not only work automatically, and are linked to each other, but that in many cases can substitute human intervention, i.e. labour power of the workers.

Last but not least, the Google Car is able to interact with the environment in which it moves to reach its destination by avoiding obstacles, respecting the rules of the road, and using the quickest route.

We can see here the progressive emancipation of the technological device with respect to the necessity that there is for constant input from the human being. This device becomes more and more capable of self-sustainment and the ability to independently interact with other subjects. This sets it apart from the technical tool. The latter, in fact, depends on the initiative taken by the human being and is constantly subjected to our control. Instead, both the clock—when charged—both the factory system, both the Google Car, although in a different way, do not depend on us to be able to work and to achieve their goals.

Technology then, as a technical system, is able to develop an act that is largely independent of human action, and by which human action must in turn do the math. Technological equipment, especially the more sophisticated ones like robots, are able to interact with the environment within which they carry out their activities and, in some cases, even "learn" from the interactions they have with the environment. Above all, they are able to take the initiative, at least for the purposes for which they were programmed. With all of this the human being interacts.

For this reason we can say that throughout history there has not been a simple linear development between technical tools and technological devices, but a real shift in the paradigm. As for our example, it is possible to argue that, contrary to what appears in Kubrick's movie, there is a substantial difference between the bone used as a weapon by the ape and the spaceship. Technique and technology are not at the same level.

In this book I will deepen the difference between technique and technology in specific areas. I will focus specifically on the context of the information and on that of communication. My analysis will aim to understand and to guide our behaviour. But first I have to clarify which are precisely the techniques and technologies of information and communication mostly used throughout the history.

## 1.2 Techniques and Technologies of Information and Communication Processes

Today we live in an era in which our ability to inform and to be informed, and to develop a real communication between us, as human beings, does not depend only on our own initiative. Today we live in an environment where information and communication processes often occur automatically, without there being on our part the desire to activate them every time. This subtracts more and more these processes from our control and ensures that they can be conceived as a real environment, a sort of "infosphere" in which we live and with which we interact (Floridi 2013, 2014).

It is an environment in which the flow of information and communication are developed according to very precise dynamics and follow laws that can be studied and measured. Such a situation has never occurred in the past, at least not with the same amplitude and pervasiveness with which it does today. We will shortly give some examples to this regard, with reference also to the tools that we use every day in this environment. By taking into account the diversity of these instruments nowadays we cannot simply talk of techniques, but of information and communication technologies (ICTs abbreviated).

What is it about? The ICTs relate, in general, to the treatment and transformation of data that are transmitted in the information processes. This data are retrieved, stored, processed, transmitted by a sender, so that they can be correctly received by a recipient. Technological development has made these processes very fast, global, pervasive, and abundant. This causes, among other things, problems that must be addressed from an ethical point of view.

Of course, in the history of mankind, we have always used specific techniques to enhance our information and communication skills, and to extend it in space and time. Think about the function exercised by musical instruments in the extension of the scope of sounds in space, for example, in primitive and prehistoric eras (Sachs 2006). However, the use of electronic technologies linked to developments in information science and the spread of computer networks has changed this scenario substantially.

We can compare the two concepts ("technique" and "technology") by using some examples of both technical and technological developments of information and communication. These examples all relate to the writing, reproduction and reading of human speech. I will analyse the processes that characterize an increasingly complex "mechanization" of speech (Ong 2012).

The spreading of writing, that is, the ability to conserve and put information in a permanent form, by using signs that represent the sounds of the spoken language, but also that of music, or specific formulas (math, logic, etc.), has certainly made it possible to process information in a different way compared to how the process was done via oral communication. The philosopher Plato was the first to notice this. At the end of his dialogue *Phaedrus*, he pointed out the fact that, because of the introduction of writing, the memory of human beings would have a minor role, since what had to be memorized in the past could now be simply written (Plato 2005, 274 c–275 b).

However, the technique of writing remained under the control of its users, even when it meant the development of additional techniques. Writing could in fact be used or not, that is, it was not replaced but simply added to the verbal skills that already existed. This technique then needed to be learnt, as did the reading technique that decoded it. Also the written text demanded of who practiced reading the development of further expertise and above all a greater understanding of what one was reading compared to what one understood in a conversation. In fact, when we are involved with the written word, it is not possible to verify our understanding of it as in a conversation with a person in front of you.

The writer and the reader must therefore develop two parallel and complementary techniques. The reader's technique is to decode and understand the written text in order to interpret it correctly. Along with the ability to write and to read a text one must therefore also develop the technique of interpretation. Together with the interpretation technique it is necessary to elaborate a more general reflection that is able to establish, and to fix in a doctrine, the correct criteria for interpretation. This doctrine is called "hermeneutics" (Ferraris 1996).

Nonetheless, in ancient times and during the Middle Ages writing techniques allowed for a limited number of elaborated and reproduced documents. Even the readers were few. In the mid-fifteenth century with Johannes Gutenberg's invention of the movable type printer an even greater separation between the production activities of a text and the possibility of reading it became evident. The writer no longer gave his writings only to the reader, but now it was handed over to the printer first, whose job was to print copies for many other possible readers than before. Furthermore, the fact of being able to reproduce mechanically numerous copies of the same written text brought forth a series of consequences for the readers themselves. These readers became more, not only because there were many more books available, but also because the text was printed, which made it easier to read than a handwritten one. Consequently there was a greater opportunity to obtain knowledge and information, and an ever greater possibility of sharing knowledge.

However, this diffusion of culture continued to be dependent on the initiative of human beings. It was an initiative dictated for example by economic reasons (like the one that pushed Gutenberg to create his invention), or by the increase in the need of knowledge, or the mere reference to the "pleasure of reading the text" (Barthes 1975). The flow of information was still limited, since it depended on the number and distribution of printed books, as well as the ability of those who took to reading it. It is true that a single book could be reproduced in numerous copies and could be read by many people, but it remained in the possession of the reader, its contents could not be modified and information regarding those who had chosen to read it, then, were not immediately shared. In short, once the book was bought, it remained under the control of the reader.

But today the situation is different. Today storage, handling, data transmission is something that has very pervasive and invasive effects. This is reflected, for example, also in the processes of diffusion of written texts and their use by readers. Today we are constantly immersed in flows of information made of sounds and images, and not only by spoken or written words. These flows engage us and overwhelm us without requiring on our behalf any specific expertise and creating a situation where we are not able stop them. The user-friendliness of this action is indeed in direct proportion to the impotence that we feel in relation to these processes.

This occurs because, today, information and communication are not only dependent from specific techniques, but are developed through the use of particular technologies. It is relevant to technologies that operate precisely through the transmission of information. Today, in fact, the processing and transformation of information is not only the result of a process, but it is the way in which the machine works.

Moreover, not only do these machines transmit data, and are programmed to do so, but they are specifically able to transmit it in a fast and computerized manner, proving to have an ever growing memory capacity and acting in conjunction with each other. As a result, and in connection with their work, our ability to inform, communicate and learn also changes. Today it is not necessary to have constant human *input* to initiate an information process as it used to be, and how it still is for those who write something, even on the computer, or that read for example a newspaper. Nowadays we can no longer only *make use of machines*, but we have to *interact with them* via the procedures and activities of those systems that to a certain extent demonstrate a certain degree of autonomy.

All of the above may be verified if we continue to follow the example of writing and reading, and if we now analyse the possibility that we have of reading a book on an electronic device after downloading it from a platform. The text in question can in fact be downloaded, sent to other readers, shared, modified and commented on infinitely. This behaviour, sometimes liable to copyright, is still a possibility, even though laws are made to safeguard it, but without success. In addition, in relation to the changed structure of the text and its technological processing, our behaviour changes with respect to the text itself. We can manipulate and transform it individually or together with other people. We can exchange it with other readers, using the same support, and our comments on it.

However, there is no way to interact only with this particular product. When we buy a book online the system takes into account the whole set of products to which it belongs, for example with other texts from the same author or on the same topic that is recommended and our preferences. We end up having to interact at the same time with the whole area in which these texts are inserted, as, for example, with the site from which we downloaded the text and to which we have provided some information in doing so. All data relevant to what we have looked for is stored and reproposed to us for any future searches. The same goes for our opinions and our interventions, such as underlining and editing the text we are reading. This data is preserved and can be publicised regardless of our will. All this not only entails particular management issues related to the storage and processing of the data, which is in an ever-increasing number, but also it implies legal and ethical problems regarding their acquisition and their possible use. We will talk about it widely later.

## 1.3 Information and Communication

Previously we stated that information and communication technologies, as generally considered as such, are those technologies that make it possible to process and transmit data through telematic channels and networks. In this case we speak about "information" and "communication" in an undifferentiated way. We talk about "information" and "communication" in the case of a whole series of technological tools that work through data transmission and that operate in order to transmit data. We use the same words "information" and "communication" indifferently to characterize one of the most commonly used activities by women and men, which is linked to the capacity of speech, of *logos*, and that according to Aristotle essentially characterizes human beings (Aristotle 1998, I, 1253 a, 9–10).

However, this identification of information and communication is not correct. Or, better, it is the result of accepting a thesis that has a precise origin and can be thoroughly discussed. It is a matter of "informing" and "communicating" which generally involves the transmission of a message, or a series of data or information, from an issuer to a receiver. Starting from this central idea of transmission, computers and humans work in the same way, and we end up talking about communication both in these cases, and in that of for example of railway communications (thanks to which wagons carrying people or goods are transferred from one place to another).

When was the thesis of the identity of information and communication born? It started to spread during the late '40s, primarily with the publication of *The Mathematical Theory of Communication* by Shannon and Weaver (1949). These authors, respectively an engineer and a probability mathematician, elaborated a communicative model of the theory on information that develops in a linear way, it establishes the various components of a communicative process and defines the form, as in the case of data transmission from an issuer to a receiver by means of a signal. In the case of a specific transmission, the *signal* is *encoded* by a *transmitter*—for example, in the case of a radio broadcast the sound waves are transformed into electromagnetic waves and can travel through a channel even at great distances. Along this path the signal may be disturbed or distorted, which needs to be as little as possible. In the end, the signal is received by a receiver that decodes the pulses transmitted at a given frequency. In this way, if we want to continue with the example of radio technology, they become perceived by the human ear.

The Shannon and Weaver model considers the communication process as an efficient transfer of information and provides a mathematical elaboration of it. For this purpose, the meaning is not taken into account, and the idea of data transmission is privileged. What is certainly justified, however, from a engineering point of view, is less so if we consider that this model becomes the reference model—the standard model—for any type of interaction not only informative but also communicative, including one that characterizes the complex activity of humans.

The introduction of this model as a standard model occurs in the context of linguistics and therefore receiving an important sense of legitimacy outside the sector of telecommunications. The language theory developed by one of the most important representatives of 20th-century linguistics, Roman Jakobson, proves this point. According to Jacobson, language is a tool that primarily fulfils a specific function. This is precisely the function for which the *sender* sends a *message* to the *receiver*, using a particular *channel*, referring to a particular *code* and moving within a specific *context* (Jakobson 1963). As mentioned before, also in this case communicating generally means transmitting information and its action is similar to that of sending a letter, postal package or transmitting a radio signal.

But why does the model of data transmission in this historical period impose itself both in the field of engineering and in the field of language disciplines, identifying information and communication? Simply because in those years, as an expression of a common sense and a mind-set that is still spreading more and more, a comprehensive project was developed based on the management, processing and control of information. This is the project that helped start a new discipline: *cybernetics*. In 1948, Norbert Wiener's book entitled *Cybernetics, or Control and Communication in the Animal and the Machine* (Wiener 2013) was published. The book exposes a theory that coordinates and integrates the investigation into human beings and that on machines. Its purpose, as the title of the book says, is to gain control over both. The condition for this control is to interpret both machine processes and the behaviour of animals as forms of communication, and consider communication as a transmission of information so that it can be computed.

Today, in the era of computers and communication networks, this general project, which at the time of Wiener was largely the result of a brilliant anticipation of what was to come, that now has become reality. Today, the "helmsman"—*kybernetes*, according to the Greek word that Wiener uses to name the new discipline—is really able to control a world in which it is difficult to distinguish between what is natural and what is artificial. That is why the concept of communicating as data transmission and its identification with information processes seem to have been acquired.

Everything nowadays is considered to be information. Computer science is the discipline that deals with these processes. The communicative activity of the human being can be rebuilt, controlled and reproduced starting from this model.

Instead, "communicating" is something different to "informing". We can verify this if we refer to our daily experience. We can see it when this is theorized by the concepts of language and communication that have been developed in the ancient world, and which are now being put in debate by the theories of engineering and cybernetics.

Let's start with this second aspect. Two great rhetors of the ancient world, Marco Tullio Cicerone (106–43 BC) and Marco Fabio Quintiliano (35–95 AD), often used the term *communicatio*, "communication", in a meaning that could also be translated with the expression "participative communication", meaning a communication, which requires active participation and involvement of the various subjects of a conversation. As some authors point out (for example Manetti and Fabris 2011), this use is related to the tradition of rhetorical thinking and is clearly expressed by Aristotle (1926, I, 1358 a, 37–b 2).

All of this emerges several times from our daily experience, to the extent that we reflect on the various aspects of our communication activity. Conveying content and giving information is certainly one of the forms of this activity. But in it and through it something more happens. A connection is made with all those who are involved in a communicative process that these subjects themselves contribute to building and consolidating. In other words, not only is something transmitted through communication, but it is also set up and maintained to the extent that this same transmission can be accomplished and continued over time. Communicating then, more generally, means spreading and promoting a common space among the various interlocutors.

In communication there is in fact an involvement that is assumed and, from time to time, reconfirmed in the exercise of communicating itself. This is an engagement in which every user of a means of communication—that is, every "locutor"—is immediately considered an "interlocutor". In other words, it is not just the sender of a message, nor the one who receives it. It is rather a subject that cooperates with the opening of a communicative context, contributing to its activation and maintenance. Anyone who is involved in such an activity is therefore a potential creator of communication. Every communication, in fact, is by itself creative.

Within this more general background, an information activity is also held. In order for it to be happily implemented, it must refer to the existence of that shared dimension whose communication is expression and fulfilment. And yet the information transmission activity is only a partial and unilateral aspect of that communicative dimension. In the information model, the initiative is always taken by the issuer, and the receiver can only respond with feedback after sending the message. In the most general case of communicative activity, however, interaction takes place consistently, the answer is somehow anticipated in order to reach an understanding and to build a common space. In short, while the information transfer model can be summed up in the image of an arrow that moves in one direction and wants to hit its target, that of shared communication is expressed by the image of a network which connections are all potentially related to everyone else. Be careful, though. This network is not first built and then used, as in the case of telecommunications networks, but is woven and put into operation through the action of communicating.

In conclusion, we can consider the term "communication" in the way it is used within the various European languages and in its etymology. In fact, the word originally derives from Latin *communicatio* and in general it is used with the meaning of "to make others participate" in what we possess. In this notion, reference is made to the metaphor of "participation", which is even more explicit in the German term *Mitteilung*, meaning "communication", precisely, as "sharing". *Communico* then means, etymologically, "to share", "to put together", and "to agree". Conceived in this way, as Benveniste observes (1966), this action indicates what is the foundation of a community (*communitas*), which means the possibility of making something of common possession *(communis)*.

It therefore has a profoundly political value. What is common then, always according to Benveniste, are *munia* or *munera*: those "gifts" belonging to the same community are exchanged with confidence to consolidate their relationships. And among these gifts the word, or more generally the communicative act, is what most effectively achieves this purpose.

## 1.4 General Ethics and Applied Ethics

The gift of communication, the *munus* of *communicatio*, may be hazardous as occurs with other aspects that characterise human beings. This danger may be used to influence other people's activities by doing them good or hurting them. We are responsible for how we use communication and the positive or negative effects it may have. This often causes a sense of dilemma. Here is an example:

If a friend shares a secret with me that is about another person, I suppose it is because he believes that I will keep the secret to myself. It could be that this information may be relevant to something that may hurt others if it is something that no one knows. Let's say this person has AIDS and the fact that it has not changed his lifestyle could cause a dilemma for me. If I tell other people his secret it will cause problems for him and consequently my interlocutors will lose their trust in me, because I don't know how to keep a secret. On the other hand, if I don't say anything I automatically become responsible for anything bad that may be a consequence of this friend's behaviour. Whatever my action is, it is a form of communication or that was avoided or that was produced. The information that is shared through this communication is an act of something good or bad, or something appropriate or inappropriate.

This happens because communicating is a form of action. In fact nowadays we refer to this as "communicative action" (Habermas 1985) and there is a distinction among the various acts of communication analysed in the field of pragmatics (Austin 1975; Searle 1970). This discipline works side by side with other disciplines that study for their part other aspects of language, such as semiotics (the study of signs and symbols) and semantics (the study of meanings).

As mentioned above, every form of action may be "good" or "bad", "right" or "wrong", "correct" or "incorrect" depending on the intentions and consequences of this action. "Good" and "bad", "right" and "wrong", "correct" and "incorrect" express an opinion about these intentions and consequences. Our choices are produced via these opinions and more in general we orientate ourselves in the world around us where we act and interact with others. A reflection on all these aspects is the task of ethics.

Ethics is generally considered as the discipline that studies the criteria and principles of action, which help distinguish good principles from bad ones, which gives guidance in the choices one may have to make, motivating us to make a good choice rather than making one that is conceived as bad. There are certainly different ways in which, in the history of ethics, but also in the contemporary debate, these various tasks are carried out. Nonetheless, during this history and in this debate, ethical questions are constantly being repeated, such as the following: What am I doing? What should I do? What is the meaning of my action?

These are basic questions that help us understand how human beings can orient themselves when acting. Also, today, doctrines that try to answer these questions usually do so on the basis of two needs. On the one hand, the need is to make a theoretical reflection upon this action and its criteria, on the concept of "good" and, more generally, on the way in which we use our moral vocabulary and, finally, on the scenarios and dilemmas that may affect our choices. This reflection develops specifically as an analysis of the language of ethics and during the twentieth century it was referred to as "meta-ethics". On the other hand, the need is to move from the knowledge and the enunciation of ethical principles to their effective implementation. It results from questions related to the application of moral criteria to concrete cases concerning the education and the formation of a virtuous character, which aims at the realization of a meaningful act. These issues cannot be resolved solely by elaborating a theory of moral behaviour. On the basis of this requirement, so-called "applied ethics" has been elaborated since the second half of the last century (Fabris et al. 2018).

Briefly I would like to take into account these fundamental questions and these various strategies which are used when dealing with issues related to our moral behaviour. We can schematically rebuild within the contemporary landscape some fundamental lines of ethics. For a complete discussion of the subject see for example the book edited by Singer et al. (2006).

First of all let's consider how there are reflections that develop from the idea of a particular structure that would be relevant to a human beings action or even, with a similar approach, to a specific "nature" of the moral object. In such cases, the goodness or the wickedness of an action would be defined according to the understanding of the nature of the good and the manner in which the human action conforms to that nature (Foot 2001). In this view, some aspects of Aristotle's ethics are discussed.

There are doctrines, however, that define good actions by referring to a series of duties that human beings recognize and to which they are obedient. The main historical reference, in this case, is no longer the Aristotle's way of thought, but that of Kant. This is the case, for example, of those authors who recognize the "language of morals" (Hare 1991) as a purely prescriptive function. A normative point of view is taken here with regard to action. Although it remains to be justified the reason why it is necessary to obey the duties that are imposed thereby.

There is then an explanation of the moral action that guides the human being as a criteria that one takes into account referring to the best consequences of such an act. These consequences can be defined individually or collectively. The privileged perspective, however, is that of consequentialism. Such an explanation of moral action falls under utilitarian doctrines (Eggleston et al. 2014).

Finally, there is the idea that living ethically involves the need to shape one's own character, to make our attitudes flourish, and therefore to realize our own life according to virtue. This is the case of virtue ethics, a form of ethics elaborated by Aristotle and reproposed by G.E.M. Anscombe during last century. From this point of view, ethics, especially in the version given by M. Nussbaum in recent years, contributes also to the flourishing of the capabilities that are characteristic of each individual (Nussbaum 2011).

In conclusion, in order to complete the panorama of contemporary ethics, it is now necessary to refer, as I have already said, to the so-called "applied ethics". It was born and affirmed in the second half of the twentieth century by trying to give an answer to the real issues that, from time to time, technological developments and their consequences positively address humans behaviours. Just to deepen and evaluate the impact of emerging technologies in the various areas of our lives, we have been spreading, for example, disciplines such as bioethics, environmental ethics, economic ethics, social ethics, ethics of communication (Cohen and Wellman 2014).

In all these cases, the concept of "application" certainly indicates the concrete ground from which the questions about our behaviours arise, but also expresses the need not to be limited to a sectorial discussion of the problem. To make those decisions that we are faced with by the ever-increasing incidences of technology on our lives (and, for example, the processes related to birth and death), we need to refer to principles that can be justified only on a higher level. In short, the idea of "application" certainly refers to the realities of problems that need to be addressed by the possession of well-defined skills: those offered to by biomedical disciplines, economic sciences, environmental research, communication practices, and so on. But it also indicates that, for their solution, provisions should be made for a more general elaboration and foundation plan, the one provided by a general ethical reflection.

However, this does not mean that in the field of applied ethics there is a mechanical application of general behavioural criteria in individual cases. On the contrary, practitioners of applied ethics know well that in a particular domain emerging issues can also put into effect universally valid principles, if they are assumed in a too abstract way. At the same time, however, they are also aware that, in order to properly base their choices, it is necessary to refer to ethical models capable of establishing the latest reasons for such choices.

There is, in fact, a virtuous circle, a mutual recall and the need for mutual cooperation between applied ethics and general ethics. General ethics elaborates and discusses patterns of behaviour that apply to all human beings and in all situations. Applied ethics, which are based on the paradigms of general ethics, allow to test these paradigms and offer concrete verification. We will see how this happens in the case of ethical issues in the ICTs.

## 1.5 Ethical and Deontological Approaches to Information and Communication

In the previous paragraph we defined the main directions in which contemporary ethics and the articulations of it are moving. The same scenario is reflected in the specific action taken through the use of new technologies, in our case, through ICTs. However, in this context of application, there is an important transformation. Ethics is called here to deal no longer with human activity alone, but with human action that is enhanced by technology. From the moment that the same technologies are now able to promote specific and autonomous actions (Scharff and Dusek 2003; Dusek et al. 2006), ethics must also deal with the criteria that guide the same technological action and interaction of humans with new artificial agents. We can take into consideration disciplines now consolidated as Machine ethics and Roboethics (Wallach and Allen 2009).

It is therefore necessary to link this situation of technological transformation to research developed by contemporary ethics (Otto and Gräf 2017). In today's debate, this is accomplished mainly by following two paths. On the one hand, ethical reflection is promoted by those that are the reference values inherent to technological action. On the other hand, we try to identify certain precise, clearly stated norms, from which it is possible that the human being is orientated and chooses when using certain devices, especially in a professional activity. In the first case, it is about developing technology *ethics* which are really appropriate to the changes made by ICTs to our behaviours. In the second case, however, we come across a more *deontological* approach.

As for the first necessity, to develop a true ethic of emerging technologies, it is necessary, as I have said, to consider that the reference ethical values today are not just those relating to human actions, but are also the ones inherent to actions performed by technology. Technologies, in fact, are not ethically neutral. There are, in them, embodied values, which are implemented in the actions that are made by technological devices, conceived in their increasing autonomy. There are, for example, embedded values within the same computer systems, independently from the particular ways they are used (Flanagan et al. 2008). From this point of view, technological artefacts are capable of either promoting or arming the realization of values when they are used.

We can see an example of this situation if we analyse the consequences of the use of communication technologies on inter-human relations and, more specifically, in the current political context. There is no doubt that these technologies favour the spreading of ever-expanding forms of sharing and participation, and so these, alongside others, are the values they carry. This results in a transformation of the very exercise of democracy and the ways in which it can be realized. Concrete not only is the possibility of "Arab Spring", as it happened a few years ago, but also that of a populism driven through the use of communication technologies. Also in relation to this ambiguous way of achieving values that are inherent to technological processes, a "disclosive computer ethics" was recently developed, which purpose is to identify the morally opaque practices in computer technology, "describe and analyse them. So to bring them into view, and to identify and reflect on any problematic features in them" (Brey in Floridi 2010, 51).

In the context of a technological ethics, the normative approach that characterizes much of modern and contemporary debate is re-emerging. It does, however, undergo significant transformations. ICTs, in fact, change our old practices, change our ways of acting, and therefore it becomes difficult to implement their own rules from a single and absolute moral principle which application is considered an unconditional duty. We must rather take into account the pluralism of values that is right from our time and to consider the difficulty of immediately applying general normative criteria to concrete situations. It is appropriate, in other words, to develop a concept that is "*empirically informed, realistic and practical*, so as to provide guidance and direction in cases where information technology is actually used" (van den Hoven in Floridi 2010, 61; more in general see May and Delston 2015).

This realistic and practical conception is traditionally provided by a deontological approach. In the history of ethics the word "deontology" has had different meanings. Bentham, for example, calls "deontology" the utilitarian doctrine that aims to coincide with interest and duty, in view of the achievement of the greatest happiness possible by most people. In the German area, however, the term "*Deontologie*", especially with reference to Kant, is used to indicate the doctrine that prescribes obedience to a duty irrespective of the consequences that result from its implementation. However, in the various contemporary cultural contexts, the word "deontology"—from Greek *to deon*, which means precisely "duty"—more properly it defines the set of duties that must be respected by those exercising a specific profession.

With the emergence of the deontological aspect, conceived in the latter way, one outlines the need for regulation of our behaviours by identifying a series of specific rules. This approach also covers the fields of information and communication, and is reflected in the listing of specific duties. More precisely, these are duties which, in a different way, concern those who carry out professionally the activities of information and communication, and those who are not professionals in the sector (since communication activity is a characteristic of being human and today we are all connected to each other through various devices) and finally those who are the object or target of the information and communication processes (that is, particular categories of people or a certain audience).

The purpose of deontology is to establish the limits of informative and communicative activity through the indication of specific regulations and prohibitions. Not all, in fact, can be communicated. Precisely because this activity has a number of consequences, it is necessary to have clear what can be communicated and what does not. For example, we consider issues related to respect for privacy or not.

In the field of communication, however, these limits cannot be imposed from the outside as this would be a censorship. Freedom of information and communication is one of the foundations of Western democracies. However, the limits that are indispensable to establish must then be the result of self-regulation by those same subjects who engage in information and communication activities. The aim is to safeguard freedom of expression together with the awareness that the exercise of that freedom must also be a responsible exercise.

The list of the various duties I mentioned is contained in the so-called "deontological codes". They offer concrete indications of behaviour, mostly in the form of prohibition, in which it is established what is legitimate that the communication operators are doing and what is not. In these codes there are also indicated the sanctions that can be met by those who transgress them. These codes, as I have said, are self-regulatory codes, and are processed by a certain professional category, such as journalists or advertisers, computer engineers or bloggers. Some of the exponents of this category, identified usually by means of elective instruments, can be those who supervise the application and who are able to punish any transgression.

However, neither these codes nor the generally accepted professional deontology can solve all the problems concerning the ethics of information and communication. In fact, the application of the regulations contained in the code of ethics is sometimes complicated and cumbersome. Very often the penalties for offenders are not a deterrent to avoid bad behaviour. This is even more apparent, as we shall see, in the field of ICTs deontology. To follow in person and to enforce the codes, one must therefore refer to a strong ethical motivation, which is the basis of the choices of individual professionals.

Yet, the code limit applies to their own structure. In fact, they provide, clearly, responses formulated in terms of legal issues to issues of a purely ethical nature. But, again, the formal fairness or the legality of certain acts does not fully coincide with their moral justification. Ethical issues concerning the freedom and responsibility of the human being cannot be addressed only by obeying a set of regulations. That is why it is necessary to develop a true ethics of information and communication (ICE) also with regard to ICTs.

## 1.6 Using Techniques, Interacting with Technologies, and Living in Technological Environments

Deontology provides assistance in understanding better what it means to do well when we operate within certain professional areas and, more generally, when we use technical tools or technological devices. Deontological codes and, in a broader sense, codes of conduct, offer us a list of regulations that can guide us by section in our concrete practices. Ethics, on the other hand, has a more general ability to guide us in our actions.

This happens for two reasons. On the one hand, it deals with criteria and principles of behaviour that are relevant to the human being considered as such and not just as a professional or user of a given device. On the other hand, ethics is the field in which the customs and habits of humans develop and consolidate through reflection and questions that concern those motivated relationships that humans themselves implement in a given context. It is no coincidence that the Greek term *ethos*, from which the English word "ethics" derives, means "habit", "costume", both conceived in both individual and collective meanings.

In this book, which will develop specifically the ethics of information and communication technologies (ICTs), I will deal with both deontological and ethical aspects. The term "ethics of ICTs" must in fact be understood in a broader sense, including both the particular requirements and the attitudes and customs that develop in our relationships within technological environments. In fact, we act within these environments, using the tools and the equipment that are part of them. We act in them, if we stick to the subject of this book, in the forms of information and communication. Such action is generally oriented by ethics and regulated in some respects by ethics.

This is, however, an act that, as we have seen, is different, more or less incisive, more or less controllable in its consequences, depending on the type of instruments or devices we are dealing with. One thing is using a technical tool, another is how we interact with technological devices, another is how we live in an environment that is increasingly characterized by devices able to relate to each other even independently of the intervention of human beings. In these three cases, changing the mode of action naturally also changes the task that ethics has.

In the case of the use of technical tools, the reference action is above all human action, which, as we have seen, is strengthened through tools. The example that I made earlier was that of the ape in Kubrick's *2001: A Space Odyssey* and its use of a simple bone as a weapon. In this case, the ethics that must be elaborated, the ethics of technique, is a derivation of traditional ethics, which was conceived as an in-depth and justified criteria and principle of the action of human beings. The technical tool depends in fact on the use made of it by this being and how it is placed under its control. The fact that this tool increases its strength and its power produces a number of further issues, but it does not change the characteristic of the action, which remains linked to a human initiative. The increase in power and the extension of the radius of this action requires a more precise regulation of the use of technical instruments, which is provided by professional ethics and codes. The professional activity depends on the proper and correct use of certain tools.

Today, however, these instruments are not only technical instruments but also, often technological devices. Therefore, as we have seen, the way in which the human being behaves in relation to such devices changes. This is because technological devices in turn take action, even with some autonomy. As a result, we not only use them, but we have to interact with them. Taking action is becoming more and more interlinked, by involving human and artificial forms of acts.

As we have seen, just taking into account this fact and the "embedded values" that technological action entails, there is the possibility of developing an ethics of technologies in the subjective sense of the genitive, which means an ethics that concerns the same activity of technological devices. On an anthropological level, then, human action that is accomplished by technological devices, for example a smartphone, is not merely an act that is able to use them and to fully control the consequences—such as those inherent in its ability to provide, if activated, a geolocation. But it is more precisely defined as an interaction with the action that is precisely of these devices. This, of course, has consequences also on a deontological and ethical level. This applies first and foremost to information and communication technologies.

Finally, considering the fact that technologies today can no longer be considered as simple tools and not even devices with a certain autonomy, but are in their interactions with each other and with us in a real environment—an artificial environment, in which we move, operate, produce—then even with respect to the aspects of information and communication we can no longer speak of "techniques" or "technologies". We must also use other words that are better suited to clarify the situation we are experiencing and to express the ethical challenges that it involves.

It can help us initially focus this situation on the original proposal for Information and Communication Ethics (ICE) that has been advanced by Luciano Floridi. Floridi starts from the fact that today we live in a decisively new reality compared to the past, which he calls "infosphere". In this reality, characterized by increasingly engaging and global information and communication flows, the role and function of the moral agent also changes compared with the past. In order for the moral agent to be able to orient itself in such a situation, Floridi formulates four fundamental laws, which essentially serve to avoid the entropy of the system in which he or she has to operate. Here are these laws: "(0) entropy ought not to be caused in the infosphere (null law); (1) entropy should be prevented in the infosphere; (2) entropy should be removed from the infosphere; (3) the flourishing of informal entities as well as of the whole infosphere should be promoted by preserving, cultivating and enriching their properties" (Floridi 2010, 92–93).

I will return later on these issues and on this author. What I am now interested in is the fact that ICTs developments not only require to be governed by re-proposing the traditional questions of ethics—What am I doing? What should I do? What is the meaning of my action?—but they are primarily changing the meaning of this same discipline, as it was conceived in the past. Against these emerging scenarios, it is also necessary to broaden the possibilities and scope of ethics as such.

For this reason the next two chapters of this book will have a very precise task. They will have to deepen, from a deontological and ethical point of view, first and foremost our relationship with the technical devices and technology that we use every day. It will then be necessary to analyse, by continuing to follow both the deontological and ethical approach, the new environments of information and communication in which we now live and work.

More specifically, *the next chapter* will discuss the forms of our actions and the different ways in which we interact with some of the most widely used devices. Think for example of the computer, the smartphone, and some automated systems. We think of devices that will shortly become widely available, such as the autopilot car. We will also explore our relationship with these devices in order to understand what it means to use them in a "good" or "bad" way, and to give concrete indications relevant to this experience.

In *the third chapter*, however, the environment of information and communication technologies will be analysed and discussed, taking into account our interactions with it and the choices that we can make in relation to this background. In this environment, crossed and formed by information and communication, relationships between humans can develop on multiple levels. They can be real, they can be mediated by specific technical tools, they can be virtual. Ethics is concerned not only with behaviours within each of these levels, but also and above all in the ways—correct or incorrect, good or bad—where these same levels can be related. Especially on the last aspect, such as in the relationship between the real world and the virtual environment and the way it can be lived in a good way, I will dwell largely in the last part of the book.

## References

Aristotle (1924) Metaphysics. Oxford U.P., Oxford
Aristotle (1926) Art of rhetoric. Harvard U.P., Harvard
Aristotle (1998) Politics. Oxford U.P., Oxford
Austin JL (1975) How to do things with words. Harvard U.P, Harvard
Barthes R (1975) The pleasure of the text. Macmillan, London
Benveniste E (1966) Problèmes de linguistique générale. Gallimard, Paris
Cohen AI, Wellman CH (2014) Contemporary debates in applied ethics. Wiley Blackwell, Malden
Dusek V et al (2006) Philosophy of technology. An Introduction, Wiley-Blackwell, Malden
Eggleston B, Miller D et al (2014) The Cambridge companion to utilitarianism. Cambridge U.P., Cambridge Mass
Ellul J (1964) The technological society. Vintage Books, New York
Fabris A et al (2018) Etiche applicate: Una guida. Carocci, Roma
Ferraris M (1996) History of Hermeneutics. Prometheus, Amherst
Flanagan M, Howe DC, Nissenbaum H (2008) Embodying values in technology: theory and practice. In van den Hoven J, Weckert J et al (eds) Information technology and moral philosophy. Cambridge U.P., Cambridge

Floridi L (2013) The ethics of information. Oxford U.P., Oxford
Floridi L (2014) The fourth revolution. How the infosphere is reshaping human reality. Oxford U.P., Oxford
Floridi L (ed) (2010) The Cambridge handbook of information and computer ethics. Cambridge U.P., Cambridge
Foot PhR (2001) Natural goodness. Oxford U. P, Oxford
Gehlen A (1988) Man: his nature and place in the world. Columbia U.P., New York
Habermas J (1985) Theory of communicative action, vol 1 & 2. Beacon Press, Boston
Hare RM (1991) The language of moral. Oxford U.P., Oxford
Jakobson R (1963) Essais de linguistique générale. Minuit, Paris
Jerónimo HL et al (2013) Jacques Ellul and the technological society in the 21st century. Springer, Berlin/New York
Manetti G, Fabris A (2011) Comunicazione. La Scuola, Brescia
May L, Delston JB (2015) Applied ethics. A multicultural approach. Routledge, London/New York
Nussbaum M (2011) Creating capabilities. Harvard U.P., Harvard MA
Ong WJ (2012) Orality and literaricy. The tecnologizing of the word. Routledge, London/New York
Otto P, Gräf E (2017) 3TH1CS: A reinvention of ethics in a digital age? i.Rights.media, Berlin
Plato (2005) Phoedrus. Penguin Classics, New York
Sachs C (2006) The history of musical instruments. Dover, Mineola
Scharff RC, Dusek V (2003) Philosophy of technology. The technological condition: an anthology. Blackwell, Oxford
Searle J (1970) Speech acts. An essay in the philosophy of language. Cambridge U.P., Cambridge, Mass
Shannon C, Weaver W (1949) The mathematic theory of communication. Illinois U.P., Urbana
Singer Ch et al (1957) A history of technology. Clarendon Press, Oxford
Singer P et al (2006) A companion to ethics. Wiley-Blackwell, Malden
Wallach W, Allen C (2009) Moral machines. Teaching robots right from wrong. Oxford U.P., Oxford/New York
Wiener N (2013) Cybernetics: or, control and communication in the animal and in the machine. Martino Fine Books, Eastford

# Chapter 2
# The Ethics of Communication Devices

**Abstract** This chapter analyses our relationship with machines, and in particular with the technological devices that we use most in our everyday communication. I would like to make an in-depth examination of the relationship between human beings and a series of specific devices that are "external" to the human being itself: the computer, the smartphone, and the robot (considered as an interactive communication system). I would like to begin by introducing a brief history of the media in the last century, in which the development of these devices can be laid out and subsequently examined. An analysis will be made of their structures, their different typologies, and their latest developments. As a result, we will analyse the deontological and ethical aspects of our relationship with each of these devices. It is the least to say that the ways in which we communicate through computers, smartphones and robotic systems differs from one to the other. Thanks to the help of the computer's hardware and its various software, we are able to extend and enhance our ability to communicate, and above all, access new communicative environments. The smartphone's portability, on the other hand, helps integrate our communicative capacity by accompanying us in our activities and leisure, and modifying our perception of space and time. With the robot, however, we can interact communicatively; we can almost "talk" to it, as can other technological devices. All of these situations require that they need to be addressed in an ethical way. Firstly, I will take into consideration the consequences that the use of these devices have on our behaviour and the problems they create: with reference, for example, to the changes caused by our interaction with the computer regarding the relationships we can establish with other human beings and the very exercise of our memory, changes in the perception of space and time due to the use of the smartphone and the fact that we increasingly have to deal with artificial entities that have some sort of autonomy. At a later stage, I will identify and justify the ethical principles that allow us to behave correctly in the technological contexts in which we live.

**Keywords** Communication devices · Computer · Smartphone
Robot · Control · Autonomy · Ethics

 
A. Fabris, *Ethics of Information and Communication Technologies*,
SpringerBriefs on Ethical and Legal Issues in Biomedicine and Technology,
https://doi.org/10.1007/978-3-319-75511-3_2

## 2.1 Preliminary Considerations

One night, travelling by car, Tim Thomas, an aerospace engineer, causes a multiple vehicle collision simply because he is looking at his smartphone and texting messages while he is driving. In this accident, Tim's beloved wife and six other people are killed. Tim decides to dedicate the rest of his life to saving the lives of seven good people, trying to repair what he has done.

This is a quite simplified summary of the plot of *Seven Pounds* (2008), a movie directed by the Italian director Gabriele Muccino and featuring Will Smith as the protagonist. The whole event is triggered by the inappropriate use of the smartphone, made by an expert in sophisticated technologies such as Tim Thomas, a graduate engineer at M.I.T. However, for the protagonist, as it often happens to us, it seems impossible not to always be connected. We have our eye constantly on the smartphone even if we are doing other things and using other devices.

The beginning of the movie has much to do with what I would now like to discuss. In fact, I want to analyse our relationship with machines, in particular, with the most technologically advanced devices we use to communicate. In this chapter I will examine the relationship between human beings and a series of devices that are "external" from humans, separated from him or her and with whom he or she can interact. However, at a later stage, I will discuss another aspect of our lives in relation to these devices: the fact that they, networked among themselves and thanks to a series of programmes, are able to create a true environment in which we live as well with which we interact each day.

This is an environment that we are strongly attracted to. It seems like we cannot give up moving within it, though we are doing other things. That's why Tim Thomas, in Muccino's movie, is unable to keep his eyes off the smartphone even if he is driving, and even though he knows, of course, that he can reply to his messages later on.

We need to take into consideration two aspects of the relationship we have with technological devices. On the one hand, they are able to react more or less autonomously and are something with which we have the need to interact. On the other hand, they help create more environments than those we move in, in our offline lives. Moving from one environment to the other we end up integrating them and putting them all on the same level, everyone is part of the same way of life. So in the end, this is what the use of technological devices makes possible for us nowadays: to live in a variety of offline and online environments.

And yet, although they tend to create a stronger integration, and even if their environments are likely to blend and mix with one another, in this relationship humans and machines reconfirm their diversity. It is because they are distinct that these entities can interact or not. This distinction implies, for both humans and these machines, the ability to act at least in part on their own.

Indeed, the communication devices I am talking about are technological devices and not just technical tools. They are characterized (as I said in the previous chapter) by the ability of self-sustainment and to relate, sometimes more or sometimes less, to the various contexts in which they carry out their actions without ever having to wait for human input. We ourselves have to deal with the contexts that the technological devices help contribute in producing. We ourselves, as we have seen, are attracted to them and we can interact with them.

In this chapter, I will consider this interaction as it takes place between entities that can be separated from each other, and therefore can be mutually connected or interrupted. We are able, that is, to turn off our computer or not respond to our mobile phones. The computer, in turn, can be disconnected or can go on standby after a period of time, and the smartphone may, in certain circumstances, automatically switch off. We may also decide not to interact with an automatic communication device, or expect no response from it. Or we can use it, in a good way or a bad way. In all of these cases, however, we must be able to justify our behaviour based on shared criteria. This is the task of ethics.

In the next chapter, on the other hand, I will look at the way in which technological devices have been able and are able to set up a real communicative environment in which we move and from which it is difficult to break away. Even when we are driving the car, like Tim Thomas, or when we are at a romantic candle lit dinner with our loved one, we often cannot resist the temptation to chat or text. We feel almost an obligation, to always respond to the constant connection needs that are expressed by our device.

Up until now, I have used two different concepts to indicate the two different kinds of relationships between human beings and technological devices, which I will discuss in this and in the next chapter of this book. The two concepts are "interaction" and "integration". *Interaction* occurs between two entities that are separate and which, even when related to each other, remain separate. Such a relationship may require one or both sides to adapt, but does not affect their structure. Think of a car and our use of it, which depends on our ability to set it in motion and to drive it: when we turn off the engine it stops. *Integration* occurs between two entities that share some structural features without which they cannot work. Or, in another sense, integration is when the functioning of an entity is a condition for the functioning of the other. Think of the series of bio-medical implants without which a seriously ill person could not survive.

Obviously, when it comes to "interaction" between humans and machines, the distinction between two structures and two different ontological modalities is assumed, while in the case of "integration" this distinction is certainly more difficult to maintain, if not impossible. All of this has important implications for our issue. While in the case of interconnection between separable entities, it is always possible for the human being to interrupt the relationship and, precisely in this way, to recover the freedom to build other relations with other entities. While in the case of integration, the choice to break the link can be understood, if taken to extreme consequences, as a gesture of destruction (or even self-destruction) and may imply the cancellation of that world from which that bond depended. That is why in the bioethical environment, for example in end-of-life situations, the decision to "disconnect" faces very different and more complex ethical problems compared to the simple choice of switching off a machine.

However, a last methodological consideration must still be made. So far, I have spoken about "machines" and "devices". In the following pages, focusing always on the communicative dimension, I will refer mainly to certain objects and the way in which our lives change when interacting with them. Referring to technological devices allows us to highlight the fact that with them we can establish a very complex relationship. Often we believe that this implies only knowing how to use them, whereas on the contrary it is important to know the purpose and consequences associated with such use. Therefore, it requires an ethical competence.

In this chapter I will illustrate what this competence is by analysing human interaction with computers, smartphones, and robots that in some ways are capable of communicating. Each of these devices represents a privileged example of certain features, specific opportunities, and a number of issues that may even affect other devices. I will consider them a bit like symbols of certain trend lines that are relevant to today's technological development.

## 2.2 Conditions of Use for Communication Devices

So far, I have spoken about computers, smartphones, and robots capable of communicating. We need to understand more specifically what this is about. We need to understand how these devices communicate and interact with how we communicate. We have to analyse the various possibilities and the various scenarios of this interaction in order to elaborate true ethics of communication devices.

Let's think of a situation that is probably familiar to all of us and that we have already come across at some point in our work experience. We are at the work table, in front of our computer. We have to make a videoconference meeting.

The software that allows us to make a connection, however, does not work properly. It could be that the people on the other side of the connection are unable to connect with us. They might be middle-aged and are not the so-called "digital natives" (Riva 2014). Changing the device seems like the best solution. We decide to use an older one. To figure out why the programme isn't working properly, to locate responsibilities, to ask, or to give the right instructions we try making a call. Meanwhile, time goes by and the beginning of the meeting is delayed. Someone asks the virtual assistant on the computer for help. Someone else points out that even the smartphone is connected to the Network and it probably has the same programme that the computer is using. So we try again. On this new device, on the smartphone, the programme works. Finally, the videoconference is underway.

What have we learnt from this situation? Not only that some devices are interchangeable, as long as they have the same programme on them. But above all, we have seen that our relationship with them is based on the requirement and necessity that they work in the easiest and most intuitive way. It's the plug and play logic. Turn the device on, connect it to another, and we expect everything to work, and run smoothly. We expect that there is no need to do anything else. We hope "Whatever Works", as the title of a Woody Allen movie of 2009 suggests. We always want

"Whatever Works" in each and every situation, whether it is a device or, as in Woody Allen's case, an inter-human relationship.

We behave a bit like the sorcerer's apprentice of whom they talk about in literature and music, movies and songs (Anders 2002). In the case of my example, we do not know the causes of certain processes; we do not have a precise idea of the structure of the devices we are using and of the communication network in which they are inserted. We do not know how programmes run and function. We are like the practitioner of which Aristotle speaks in his *Metaphysics*, distinguishing himself from the scientist (Aristotle 1924, I, 1, 981 a 25–30). So if things go smoothly, often to stop them we sometimes try to block everything. If, on the other hand, there is a problem, we often react like those cartoon characters who, when their car stops they give it a kick to start the engine up again.

The main problem, however, is that we almost never worry about the purpose and consequences of our use of technological devices; we do not ask ourselves specific questions regarding it. We use them and that's it. Returning to our example, it is not relevant for the use of the technologies involved to know whether videoconferencing is used to coordinate a rescue or something illegal. In the end, all that counts is that everything works.

But we cannot make do with just this. We need to reflect on what we do. We cannot simply act irretrievably, adapt to the system, learn to use it better and integrate more and more with it. It may be that the system itself does not satisfy us. And you too, if you have chosen to read this very book, it means that you do ask yourself some of these questions. You're not at all like those who, when a new iPhone model comes out, you only feel the need to be the first to have it and queue all night, in front of the Apple Store, waiting for it to open.

Instead, for our purposes, it is good to know at least what is at stake when we are dealing with the various devices that we use for communication. This does not mean, of course, that we have the knowledge of a computer engineer, designer, or programmer. This is not what this is all about. We need to have a clear idea about what's changing in our lives because of the interaction we have with these devices. We need to understand how they affect our thinking, common mentality, and individual and shared behaviours: our habits, our *ethos*. We need to highlight and evaluate how these devices change our behaviour. This is the starting point for understanding what it means to "behave correctly" with them, through them, interacting with them, and justify the choices that we constantly make in this relationship. To do this, however, we need to pick up from the previous chapter the brief history of technology.

## 2.3 A Brief History of Media in the Last Century

### 2.3.1 *Photography, Cinema, Gramophone*

In the previous chapter on the distinction between techniques and technologies of information and communication processes (Sect. 1.2), I re-constructed the development of reading and writing activities, the reproduction of written texts and their use, by showing how the invention of a specific machine, the mobile printer, has revolutionized both the acquisition and the transmission of knowledge. All this has further development in the second half of the nineteenth century, during the Second Industrial Revolution. This impulse soon extended to all forms of communication—that is, not only written, but also spoken, not only through the means of signs, but also through images. In the course of the twentieth century its consequences became more and more vast and incisive (Briggs and Burke 2010).

These are developments that are linked to the invention of new media devices, which further increase the chances of human communication. The devices in question are not just instruments that serve to achieve a certain purpose, but are technological devices that can alter the perception of space and time, and require specific locations for the exercise of their action: for example, photographic and cinematographic reproduction devices. I'm thinking in particular of how the cinema, while being situated in a circumscribed place, allows to expand the experience of humans through the illusion of seeing in the present what is happening in other places and at other times. The cinematographic images are in fact highly endearing. They are almost perfect reproductions of reality, such as those that provide photography, but are above all characterized by movement. It thus emerges here, more forcefully than in the case of other representations, such as those offered by paintings or theatre, the need to distinguish between reality and fiction. If that does not happen, we risk being like those spectators who escape from a room because they see a train moving towards them on the screen (Gomery and Pafort-Overduin 2011).

In parallel, thanks to the gramophone and again to the cinema, the idea of endless reproducibility and endless repetition arises according to the needs of the performer, of the same media product, whether it is a song, opera, or movie. This entails the loss of its uniqueness and originality. It also implies, through this repetitive reproduction, the uniformity of its realization (although it can have different effects when used on different subjects and at different times, even if the performance remains the same). In short, with an expression that has been successfully used, there is the loss of its "aura" (Benjamin 2012).

### 2.3.2 *Cinema, Radio and Television*

With the development of the electronic media, in the course of the twentieth century, such aspects are known to have accelerated this development in an even greater integration among different devices and a massive penetration on an ever-widening audience. For example, electronic media is not just cinema, as it became integrated with sound technologies in the twenties transforming it into "talkies" (sound movies), but it is also radio and television. Radio and television used a new signal distribution system called broadcasting mode, which allowed a single broadcaster to reach countless reception points at the same time and making it available to infinite users.

This created the right conditions for a true step up in class in mass communications. It changes, in fact, the very concept of "mass", and that is why the dictatorial regimes of the twentieth century immediately took advantage of this use (Canetti 1984). The mass is made of individuals considered in the same and uniform manner. Their equality and uniformity are given by a similar reception capacity. The personal profile and the individuality of these people do not matter. What does is that they are reached by the signal and affected by what it transmits. Individuals, in the mass, are real targets. It is not surprising that, from the early thirties of the last century, in connection with this idea, scholars developed a well-defined communication theory: the so-called bullet theory (Manetti and Fabris 2011, Chap. 1).

There is another aspect to consider. While in fact, with the spread of printed media, mass communication was linked to the necessity to buy and read a newspaper, with radio and television it was just enough to simply be in possession of a receiving device. The skills required, for example to be informed, are less. You do not need to know how to decode or interpret a text: just listen and have time to watch. Thanks to the use of these devices, also the perception of time has changed. Now, you can immediately communicate, "live", what is happening without having to wait, like in the case of newspapers, where printing and distribution are done the next day. What is immediately communicated in the present seems to have more value than what needs a longer time for processing.

### 2.3.3 Digital Media

It is, however, at the end of the seventies of the last century that the change we are interested in most occurred. This is the process of digitizing information that made it possible to create new devices and a significant transformation of the old ones. This is, more precisely, the more extensive and irreversible transition from analogue communication to digital communication.

What does the term "digital" mean? It indicates how, by the use of certain technologies, sounds and images, and more generally any physical dimension, are decomposed and homogenized by transferring them to a binary sequence of zero and one. In other words, each signal is brought to this numeric sequence, encoded on it and transformed into a data packet. Computer science is the discipline that deals with the processing and management of this data. This can be done by using algorithms, which is a series of calculation procedures that solve a given problem by following a precise sequence and a set number of steps. I will go back to this concept when talking about the function of search engines (see Sect. 3.4.1).

This process of digital homogenization, however, is not something natural and desirable, even though it is a universally widespread approach to our culture. It is based on a number of assumptions and has several consequences. I have mentioned some of them in the previous chapter. Communication, in its multiple aspects and forms, from which people make experience, is identified with an information activity. Information is carried out by transmitting data from a sender to a receiver. Thus, as Wiener showed, the animal and the machine can be put on the same level and treated in the same way (Wiener 2013). The consequence is the indifferent treatment of different entities.

In other words, in a digital information context, data can easily be decomposed, manipulated or combined. Sending it is much easier than it was before and the reception much safer. Thanks to its digitization, the signal acquires more power and speed, and can be treated much more easily. So, in view of these aspects, in particular, the fact that the same digital media can connect to non-media domains, and that the contrast between "natural" and "artificial" has *vaporized*, our era has been referred to as a "post-medial condition" (Eugeni 2015).

### *2.3.4 Computer, Smartphone, Robot*

Digitization processes have decisive consequences with regard to the development of communication devices. This is especially in the case of the *computer*. The term "computer" comes from the Latin *cum-putare*: comparing data in order to draw a definite result. But computer activity is no longer merely a matter of calculating. It has in fact changed its initial function and extended its role from a calculating machine (electronic calculator) to a new communicative medium. In parallel, its size is decreasing and it has gone from business computer to "personal computer" (according to Stewart Brand). The first marketing examples of this device were introduced almost contemporarily in 1981 by IBM and Olivetti. In 1984 the Macintosh Apple was put on the market with a more user-friendly interface. This created a radical change in our behaviour, something that its producers were well aware of. They expressed the awareness of this true revolution in a popular spot that made reference to George Orwell's famous novel and concluded with the following words: "On January 24th, Apple Computer will introduce Macintosh. And you'll see why 1984 won't be like *1984*".

However, digitization of signals, that is to say, where communication is becoming more and more transformed into the transmission of information, is only one of the aspects leading to the creation of new devices and the radical transformation of the old ones. Examples of this latter case is the transition of certain commonly used devices—such as the camera, radio, television—from analogue transmission and playback modes to a digital mode. But what is this step, and more precisely, this transition?

We have already seen how the digitization of a signal is realized. To be digitized, however, it is always an electrical signal: digitization is one of the ways in which physical quantities are transformed and processed electronically. Previously, however, this processing was analogic, meaning that the electrical signals were continuous and could take on the infinite range of possible values of the magnitudes they reproduced. This was followed by a different type of signal which was discontinuous and could only assume two values of the infinite possibilities available. As I have already said, it is the presence and absence of the signal itself: zero and one. It therefore changes the way to transpose a physical magnitude—a sound, an image, etc.—into the signal, and it changes the forms of use that we have of it.

The digital revolution, as I mentioned before, invests in old and new media. However, there is another specific way in which it affects their development. In fact, in the 1980s, other significant processes occurred. There was an increase in channels for the distribution of media products and their forms of communication. Not only did television channels multiply, but the same movie could be seen in at the cinema, on TV, on a tablet, and watched again and again with a videocassette player. All of this was connected to the creation of new technological devices. In turn, these new devices, thanks to the miniaturization of circuits, they became smaller and more portable. Think of the devices used for listening to music while walking. Think of some tiny cameras. But more so, think of the phone, which went from a landline telephone to a mobile one.

All this entails a new way of dealing with these devices. They become something that can always accompany us. They are part of us. We wear them, to the point that they seem like some sort of prosthesis. But they are many, simply too many.

The problem that arises is connected to how to unify and integrate them. It is necessary to have the functionality of many devices converged into one single device. The transition from analog to digital, along with miniaturization of circuits, makes this integration possible. Thus there is the creation of devices which are programmed to perform many functions and promote various communication activities. The most widespread example is the smartphone. With it, we cannot only call, photograph, listen to music, but also do many other things.

The *smartphone* is a particularly smart and multifunctional phone, as the word itself says. This is a device that integrates a multitude of devices in one, programmed for producing and transmitting multiple contents. Most of this is related to work and entertainment. Hence, from this the whole life of a human being is affected by these communicative functions, and furthermore, its lightweight pocketsize shape has increased its success when compared to other devices like the computer, or even the laptop.

As I said before, there are so many things that we can do with a smartphone. We can broaden the range of our actions. But how? The answer to this question leads us to the third and final aspect on which I want to dwell in my reconstruction of the latest technological developments.

We saw that the computer is the device where the digitalization of the electrical signals is realized in the most significant and emblematic manner, and that the smartphone has in a certain sense "incarnated" the integration of various devices, offering the ability to enjoy, produce, and transmit all kinds of content. But neither the computer nor the smartphone could perform their functions if they are not to some extent automated systems, or more so, put together on a Network.

An automated system is not only capable of integrating several machines into a single principle of control (Diebold 1983), and is not just a system capable of self-regulation based on the tasks for which it was programmed. It is also an adaptive system. It is developed so that it can adjust itself based on the mechanisms of the other devices it is connected to and to perform a series of actions in response to the actions of these devices.

The concept of "automation" is used in general with reference to the mechanisms that are relevant to technological, social, economic, and communication domains. In the context of communication, automation processes, characterized by self-regulation and adaptation, come together with other phenomena I have already referred to, such as the proliferation of information channels and the need to link them together. It thus changes the logic of communicating: the vertical and unidirectional model of broadcasting (the one-to-many model) replaces the horizontal and multidirectional network (the many-to-many model). The conception of mass intended as the target of information is complemented by the idea of a subject that is simply part of the system, and is able to interact with the various flows of communication and produce specific content in turn.

From the point of view of communication, all this refers to those processes that, in the last decades of the twentieth century, have led to the birth of the Internet. I am talking about the creation (in 1973) by Kahn and Cerf of the Internet Protocol Suite (TCP/IP), which was adopted as a standard in 1982. It was made to improve substantially the transmission of data between different kinds of computers connected to various networks, connected in turn to Arpanet. Following this, in 1989 the World Wide Web was created, a Network of texts that refer to other texts, by following the Hypertext logic (Hypertext Transfer Protocol). Consequently, I'm referring to the various phases that the Internet has gone through: the first Internet stage of linked sites according to the logic of hypertext in which we can "navigate" like "Netsurfers", the second stage of the well-known Social Networks, within which we are not only users, but primarily content producers that telematically share data, and finally the era of the so-called "Internet of Things", in which machines are networked among themselves to communicate with each other. This is a story, however, destined to continue.

I will not dwell on these various aspects now as I will do it in-depth in the next chapter. Instead, now I want to identify the device in which, in this case, the aspects of automation and networking are the emblematic expression and represent the last element I want to highlight. This device today is the *robot*.

This word derives from the Czech language and was coined by the writer Karel Čapek. It etymologically refers to forced house work and the figure of the slave. But there are many types of robots. And not all of them fall into this meaning of subordination. What we fear today is, indeed, that there is a reversal of perspective in which the servant becomes master and takes over from who built it. This sense of fear can be found in many novels and recent movies (see for example *Ex machina* (2014), directed by Alex Garland, and many others).

However, there are many variants of these systems. Primarily we are interested in devices explicitly designed to carry out communication activities. These are systems, that is, that are not just communicative media, such as a computers or smartphones, and which are not only needed to increase our communication capabilities, but which, in certain limits and in certain ways, in turn "communicate". They can "communicate" with us and with other devices taking, with greater or less autonomy, the initiative to do so. I will deal with this in the next chapter after examining the computer, the smartphone, and how ethically and deontologically we can relate to how the robot is involved in specific communication processes. Indeed, it can be subject and protagonist, forcing us to recover and redefine the very meaning of our communication.

## 2.4 Computer Ethics and Deontology

### *2.4.1 Our Lives with Computers*

Nowadays almost everyone owns a computer. Almost all intellectual work is mediated by this device. But we also spend a lot of our free time in front of a screen and a keyboard. As far as I'm concerned, I realised I spent a lot more time with my laptop than with my wife. However, we do not always have clear ideas on how to interact with this device. We do not always have full awareness of how it changes our lives and behaviours.

We have seen that the computer is the symbolic expression of the potential of digitization and its consequences. It does it within a communicative dimension. By exploiting the potential of digitization completely, the computer has been transformed into a communication medium by a simple computing and processing tool. With the miniaturization of the circuits, it has become portable. From a desk in the office, something "personal" has happened (personal computers, namely: PCs). From something that was "on top of the desk" (desktop) it has become something that is "on our lap" (laptop). It is a device that can be carried around with us everywhere, and can even be used for taking notes (notebook), perhaps because it is possible to unplug the video from the keyboard (tablet).

Above all, as a communicative medium and because of its portability, it enhances our relationship abilities. That is, it can put us in contact with other realities and with other people. This contact is established by the Network to which the computer is connected. The various computers, in fact, are networked. And just because they are part of this reticular structure they offer always new possibilities of interaction. The computer, we might say, is a "Keymaster"—like Vinz Clortho, a character in *Ghostbusters* movie (1984)—that opens up not only some doors, but endless connections.

But the computer is not just this. It's not just a device in a network connected to other devices, it is not limited to giving us access to multiple relationships, and it does something more: it opens up a specific environment; it creates indeed environments that, without its action, would not exist. In fact, thanks to its programmes, it is able to open new contexts and interactions. These are contexts and scenarios that are now part of our daily experience, though they are the result of an extension of it. These are dimensions that do not fall into what we usually call "reality". Instead, they belong to a "virtual" dimension. The tendency to extend, which I have just mentioned, still does, in this case, also talk of "reality", specifically of "virtual reality".

I will focus on this topic in the next chapter. Here, however, wanting to understand better the use we make of specific devices, I will examine some of the features of the computer and our interaction with it by taking into consideration the concept of Information and Computer Ethics, a concept that has already produced an abundance of literature (among the most recent contributions I will just point out: Drushel and German 2011; Floridi 2010, 2013; Johnson 2009; Migga Kizza 2013; Quinn 2012; Reynolds 2013; Sanders and Brinkman 2013; Stamatellos 2007; Tavani 2012).

As far as I am concerned, within that debate, I will focus only on some aspects: the character of computer portability and its limits; the programmes your computer needs to work properly (the distinction between software and hardware); the way some of these programmes transform our communication skills, and the perception and rebuilding of our past.

### 2.4.2 *Is a Personal Computer Really Something* **Personal***?*

The computer is one of many devices that, in the contemporary world, has taken on the character of portability. From electronic computers that occupy entire rooms, it has gone from being a desktop that is on a desk and then to the laptop that is enclosed in a bag. It can be easily transported by a single person, it is small and weighs very little, and it joins together, in an integrated way, various hardware components.

Computer portability is certainly an aspect that greatly affects our relationship with it. It has enabled the laptop to become the perfect companion for many of our activities. On one hand, like all the co-workers we interact with, it has been made to adapt to our psychophysical structure, on the other hand, it requires a specific adaptation on our part.

But is it really true that the laptop is something so portable? In fact, often a pocket-sized device like the smartphone, even if it has lower performance, is preferable as the laptop's size and weight are still an issue for some. Computer portability, including the laptop, is therefore subject to structural constraints. At least in the current state of technological development, there is an inversely proportional relationship between the portability of a computer and its ability to perform its functions. The more functions it can serve, the more integrated devices it has, the greater its complexity, its size, and therefore its weight.

To solve this problem, computer makers have tried to select the main features and those most wanted by the users, and on the other hand, to find other ways to ensure their use. For example, the first process has led to the development of a very precise device such as the iPad. However, the second need has for example led to the exclusion in certain laptops of the CD and DVD players.

The iPad is a hybrid device located between the laptop and the smartphone. It would be "insanely simple" (Segall 2012, 2016). It is made so that it maintains the power of the computer while eliminating the physical keyboard and it secures the same possibilities of communication of an iPhone. It does so with the ability to use many applications (apps), with the added benefit of offering, compared to the iPhone, the convenience of a wider screen. Soon, however, the iPad turned out to be uncomfortable to make phone calls, so it ended up replacing not the mobile phone, but the laptop, just because of its light weight and portability. Given that its data storage capacity is mostly limited, it has primarily taken on the access function for databases available on the Network. Cloud computing technology, the ability to archive and process data over the Internet starting from a set of pre-existent and user configurable resources, has made it possible to achieve this. Finally, unlike most computers and again on the same level of current smartphones, the iPad has adopted the touchscreen technology. To give commands, that is, there is no need for a mouse (external or integrated, trackball or touchpad, with wires or wireless), but there is a direct, immediate relationship between our touch and the icons on the screen. In this way, the senses that are involved in our relationship with the device are no longer just the ones of sight and hearing, but also that of touch (awaiting further development in the virtual world with the use of the other senses of smell and taste).

However, the need to ensure maximum computer portability has led, however, to the waiver of certain functions. In many cases, these features are no longer managed by a dedicated component, integrated in the system, but can be obtained from an online vendor that, free of charge or by payment, provides what previously could be acquired or reproduced through this component. In other words, it is no longer necessary to buy the original or copied product and have the device that plays it, but just download it directly from the Internet. So in other words we have moved on from the logic of possessing something to the logic of using a service.

All this entails a definite change in our habits and customs. This is a change in our *ethos*, a term that indicates the individual and collective behaviour of human beings. Therefore, in this case it is more appropriate to make reference to ethics more than deontology.

In particular, what emerges is a series of well-defined trends. First and foremost, there is a constant need to make our relationship with a technological device more and more straightforward. The search for a user-friendly setup, as well as the desire to achieve greater compactness and portability of the device itself, are the obvious signs. On the one hand, this trend involves a gradual decrease in the level of expertise needed for users to interact for example with a computer, and is necessary if one wants to reach a wider range of customers. An example is Microsoft's 1995 introduction of desktop icons. From that moment on, the necessity to type strings of commands became obsolete and simply clicking on a small image was sufficient. On the other hand, all of this user-friendliness induces us to think that a device is not simply at our service, but indeed, our companion. A reliable companion, that shouldn't cause us any problems.

Finally, the computer launched the trend of sharing certain services and giving up ones individual possession of objects. What you buy and what you want to possess are the key to access a dimension where everything is present and much can be shared, depending on each individual's needs. From this point of view, the personal computer is "personal" not so much so that it is programmed to store and archive the data that I need, acquire and that become mine, but rather in the sense that it allows access, from a specific individual position, to something of common domain. As a result, "personal" does not refer to the content you obtain but the way you have access to them. It is this mutated idea of "personality" that comes to constitute my identity on the Web.

### *2.4.3 Hardware and Software*

I have already pointed out that, in order to work, the computer needs software. It is not just a machine; to operate and to perform its functions the machine needs programs. This dualism—machine and programmes, hardware and software—distinguishes the structure of the computer, i.e. defines its specific being. Computer ontology, in short, is a dual ontology.

Therefore, it is not enough to build or buy a machine. Without programmes the machine is useless. That is why manufacturing companies try to have the monopoly of certain programmes. That's why they offer those that are only compatible with certain hardware. That's why they try to impose, along with the machines they sell, certain programmes, which you obviously have to pay for. Moreover, these programmes, if the customer wants to continue to use a particular type of device, they need to be updated or even changed after a few years.

Not only the developer, therefore, but also, and above all, the programmer is essential for our interaction with the computer. For this reason, with a pinch of provocation, a few years ago the title of a book was—*Is God a Programmer?*—an analogy between God and the world, and a programmer and his computer (Simons 1988). What seems to be more valuable nowadays is not so much the creation of hardware as the processing and development of all kinds of software.

From this situation, there is a clear responsibility not only of the developer, but also and above all of the programmer. Given that his or her work offers the decisive *trait d'union* between us and the machine which we use. That is why, within ICTs, a number of levels of responsibility and specific areas in which this responsibility can be exercised were quickly identified. As a result, codes of conduct have been developed in the field of professional ethics.

The term "responsibility" in this context has essentially two meanings (Raffoul 2010: 17–18). On the one hand, it indicates the conscious assumption of those consequences of the chain reaction of one or more actions that depends on my role and my concrete participation in those actions. These consequences may, in many cases, be anticipated, and this is another element to be taken into account when determining responsibility in legal procedures. On the other hand, the term refers to the introduction of a set of fundamental criteria that I can use as guidelines for my choices, especially in cases where the consequences of my actions are unpredictable. To do so, I "answer" to principles that I am bound to. In the first case, there is an "answer for" (of the consequences of certain actions), in the second an "answer to" (the criteria and principles that guide me in doing them).

Both who designs and builds a device, and who develops and programmes it, belong to well-defined professional categories. For this reason, their actions, within the limits of the profession, are governed by specific codes of conduct. As seen in the previous chapter, they identify the duties that certain categories of operators must follow to do their jobs well. However, the codes I'm referring to can affect a larger number of people not only, as I have said so far, those who work *on* computers (designers and hardware manufacturers) and *for* computers (designers and software developers), but also those who work *with* computers, i.e. hardware and software users (or users in general). Here, however, I will focus above all on the deontological and ethical issues concerning the first two categories.

There are many ethical choices and dilemmas that the manufacturers, but especially programmers, are called on to face. They generally concern the consequences of their activity and, more specifically, the role that their professional activity plays in determining those consequences. Of this, they mainly deal with some reference codes, established by well-known professional associations.

I am referring, for example, to the ACM code (Association for Computing Machinery: www.acm.org; now–2018—under revision) and to the code approved (June 2014) by the board of Directors of the IEEE (Institute for Electronic and Electrical Engineers: www.ieee.org). These codes want to safeguard certain specific moral conditions. They are, for example, the "dignity" of all people involved in computer processes; the "personal integrity and honesty of professionals"; the "responsibility" in the exercise of their work; the "confidentiality of information"; the "public safety, health, and welfare" in the online and offline world; the "participation in professional societies to improve standards of the professions"; the idea that "knowledge and access to technology is equivalent to social power"; the fact that this social power is something that must be shared and within reach of all.

These are fundamental values welcomed by each community. Of their continuance and maintenance, I repeat, the codes mentioned above give a precise indication and guarantee. However, they do not offer the justification of the fact that these and only these are the fundamental values to be pursued, nor the concrete motivation that compel us to do so. Such instances, on the other hand, must respond to ethical reflection: for example, the ethics that are based on a shared sense of responsibility.

But just how is this responsibility articulated and how is it specifically dealt with by the various categories of professionals mentioned so far? How is it possible to distinguish the function and consequences of the various activities that are being carried out in the design, programming and development of a computer? The first thing to say about this, is that such questions are inevitable. There is always a responsibility to look for, even in the case of these activities. It is not true that the designer of a device or a programmer simply has to follow the paths already drawn by others in order to contribute to technological advancement. It doesn't mean that all that is made possible by technology is in fact also ethically legitimate. The scenarios for the future uses of certain devices and certain programmes must therefore be anticipated, as consequences deriving from this are responsibilities of the designer, manufacturer, and programmer. However, one must also be aware that not everything can be foreseen and that, very often, what is expected to happen is not realized according to expectations.

At this point, it is necessary to identify the part of the responsibility of each of the subjects involved within a particular process. This responsibility applies not only to the roles I have highlighted, like the designer and the hardware manufacturer, and the software programmer and developer. It also extends to those who market the products as well as the end users, to whom the next chapter is dedicated. As regarding who sells hardware and software there is still a consideration to be made.

It is commonly accepted that a computer can be bought and sold at a certain price. Instead having to pay for software remains under discussion. It has also been argued that in the world to which the computer gives access, that is the Internet world, the rules governing the ownership of intellectual property and the right to use and market them should be eliminated. "Copyright" was sought to replace "copyleft". And all this was done on the basis of a true ethical issue, the one that led to the elaboration of the so-called "hacker ethic" (Himanen 2010). The "hacker ethic" is based on the idea that all on-line programmes must be available free of charge, because their development and correction may be the result of collective work.

All this has certainly led, in fact, to the coexistence of a dual regime in the use of the computer. The device must be purchased; the programmes in some cases yes, in others no. And yet in other cases, only the basic versions of some programmes are available for free, while the most sophisticated and professional ones are marketed.

Here is a real ethical dilemma. It concerns, on the one hand, the need to recognize and safeguard the individual work of the mind and, on the other hand, to allow it to be used by as many people as is possible adopting the idea that everyone has the right to access the "community of communication" (Apel 1998). There is thus an instance of justice for the benefit of certain individuals, and a gift ethic in favour of the development of the whole community. This dilemma can only be solved if one takes an ethically balanced position, where an important role is played by the ancient category of "prudence". We will see it better in the next chapter, when we deal with the same issues within Social Networks.

### *2.4.4 Writing, Reading, Memory*

The most widespread programmes, those for which a computer has been and are widely used by people with little knowledge in programming, are those related to writing and reading processes. This is certainly a minimal way of exploiting the potential of this machine. And yet this is extremely indicative of how it interacts with our communication habits.

In the previous chapter we saw the impact that the writing technique has on the transmission of human knowledge. In particular, as Plato emphasized, this technique has strongly affected our memory. It was no longer necessary to remember the events precisely, as they could be put down in writing forever. The invention of mobile printing has further modified this, as we have seen, the ways of spreading writing and has changed profoundly people's reading habits. However, it has not had such a strong impact on our ability to remember, unless it is possible to store texts written in handy formats (books) and favour the spread of appropriate places for collecting, storing and consulting these texts (libraries). The use of the computer transforms our writing and reading habits in the same way, and at the same time generates, for the first time in centuries, a radical transformation in the exercise of our memory.

Regarding writing, the computer is a machine that is placed on the same level as the typewriter (mechanical or electromechanical). The computer is made more or less in the same way. It has keys with which you can write, and what is written is immediately visible, not on paper but on a screen.

In this regard, it is to be said that the habit of typing on the keys has already caused a transformation in the exercise of human ability over the system of writing using a basic technical instrument such as a pen. It is increasingly difficult today to write easily and "in beautiful calligraphy" with a pen. And it is not necessary to retrieve this habit even the ability to write freely on the screen using calligraphy recognition software.

The computer however changes our relationship with writing not only because the expression of our thoughts in writing is keyboard-driven and rendered visible on a screen. The transformation is significant because the computer is a technological device, and not just a technical tool. As such, it interacts with our actions. Therefore, we have to worry not only about what we do through the computer, but about what it does in turn: cooperating with our actions or perhaps intervening on them even against our intentions.

This is the case of "assistance". The first thing that comes to mind is that of the spell-check. In some cases, this programme is certainly very useful, because it allows us to write quickly without having to stop and check the correct spelling or order of our words. However, it is not able to check non-standard terms, such as the surname of people who, by changing a simple letter, can be transformed into a common name, and is not always flattering (as when the Italian movie director's surname "Muccino", mentioned above, is automatically corrected into "Mucchino": "little cow" in English, and so on). In this case, we are forced to read and correct what has been typed, with extra time spent in expanding the vocabulary included in the programme. Otherwise, rightly so my interlocutor can feel offended.

This example shows that, thanks to the use of the computer and some of its special programmes, our ability to write has certainly expanded, and it is easier and quicker but we are also able to modify the written text, to archive it and make it immediately available for its distribution and for printing. In fact, its format makes it easy to save it on any kind of backup device, send it by email, and transfer it to paper. On the other hand, however, to get all of this, we have to interact with a programme. It is a software that follows certain procedures. The procedure is a sequence of well-defined, repeatable, and therefore programmable steps. It involves the assumption of a series of more or less rigid rules that characterize it as such and that the procedure itself must follow in order to achieve it correctly.

This is the point: despite attempts to bring our behaviour to a number of standard procedures, human beings do not behave according to certain procedures. A person's agenda can change without reason or notice. One may even have planned not to have anything programmed (the same as when you wander around without a specific destination). In other words, the problems in interaction between human and artificial devices derive from the fact that human beings behave most often by following analog processes, while technological devices operate, as we have seen, according to digital procedures.

This leads to the need to activate a true cultural mediation between humans and machines, between what is produced by man and what the machine puts to work. At this stage, this is a task that can be carried and cared for only by human beings. In doing so, the writing activity, and the transformations it undergoes in our technological age, is an emblematic example.

A similar transformation can easily we seen in the act of reading. Even a machine can "read", as is in the case of the photocopier and the scanner. But "to read", in this case, means precisely "to reproduce", and if not interpret, finding data quickly and reorganizing it, if not understanding the reason why it may be of importance.

Once again there is a change in the interaction with the device, specifically in the action of reading, and hence its scope and its significance for us. Today there are numerous devices that we use for reading. No longer do we read on paper but on the screen. This entails a change in the ability and concrete exercise of human reading. On the one hand, in this process, there is certainly the ease of use to the extent that, for example, characters can be magnified and spaced at will. There is, however, also the lack of a precise spatial contextualization of the words on the page, and the page within the book. That capacity allows the reader to interact in only some parts or in all, and anticipate the sense of a global meaning, which is very useful for orienting and for carrying out the reading path within a text. Failure or the transformation of it, because of the use of e-book readers (or e-readers), has cancelled or somewhat modified these aspects, therefore changing our ways of reading and learning.

The most convenient aspect offered by e-readers is the fact that they allow you to download texts from virtual libraries, free or by payment, and to store a large number of books on a single portable, if not pocket-sized device. Real libraries, that require large spaces to collect volumes in, are gradually being replaced by other ways of making available the preserved cultural heritage in written form. Thus, virtual libraries are emerging where volumes, thanks to the Internet, are made available to all or part of the users of the Web. An example of this is the Google Books Library Project, which aims to create, in the future, "a comprehensive, searchable, virtual card catalogue of all books in all languages".

Even in this case, there are various consequences, sometimes in contrast with each other. If, on the one hand, so much of human knowledge is easily and comfortably reached from ones armchair thanks to the availability of an Internet connection, and if more information and news can be acquired through the use of a search engine, on the other hand, it produces less opportunity to create physical contact with a paper book, replacing it with a technological device that goes by "paperwhite" only by name. The same will happen in the case where one has to do research on a text and compare it with other texts, it is likely to be replaced by an automatic procedure, a standard option offered by the application of a particular algorithm. Nonetheless in my opinion, always with regard to the exercise of our ability to write and read, the most important consequence is the one that interests the use of our memory.

In fact, with the computer, the human being has gained extra memory much more powerful than the one that could be activated by the power of writing (first reflected upon by Plato). Manual writing allowed news, information and thoughts to be fixed and guarded on any kind of support whether it was stone or paper. And the same thing happened with print-writing, dramatically increasing the spread of a text. In the case of technological writing, that is, of computer-generated video-writing, it is possible to save what has been processed without needing to print it. In this way, once we have written and saved a text, we feel like we have lost the obligation to remember its contents. We have an external memory, where these contents are stored and can be retrieved if needed.

But there is also something more that can be guaranteed by the computer. The new element, as far as memory usage is concerned, is represented not only by the ability to store data, on the computer or on-line, much more than what a human being can do, the novelty is mainly due to the fact that this ability to store data combines the possibility of having access to it, connecting with it and linking it altogether. Memory, therefore, is not only external, but is accessible in different ways than those normally used to obtain it.

This bond between data storage and our connection to it completely changes the scenario. Therefore, Plato's reflections cannot help us in this case. The connection is not left to the human being (already overwhelmed by the need to store notions), but is also provided in many cases by machine procedures. In other words, if the exercise of memory implies selection and conservation processes, these processes themselves can now be delegated to something external, on which the human being has no full control and with which we must interact. There is a growing emphasis on "cognitive outsourcing" (Ahlstrom-Vij 2017; see also Ahlstrom-Vij 2013).

That is why the transformations in writing and reading produced by the computer have consequences that go beyond this same act. This is another example of situations in which human beings are called upon to operate nowadays. One must do so by mediating between the two extremes of the refusal of technology and the blind adherence to it, and in some ways dehumanizing in certain procedures.

For this purpose, it is certainly necessary to elaborate specific ethical criteria. But it is still required, on an anthropological basis, the adaption of our capabilities to these scenarios. As writing began to raise awareness of the need for interpretation, so the spread of storage and connection technologies requires the cultivation of new skills. Among these is the acquisition of some basic knowledge, the ability to critically evaluate the available data, the ability to find, for each content, alternative ways of searching and linking it together. Teachers need to involve their present and future students in developing these new skills.

## 2.5 Smartphone Ontology and Ethics

### *2.5.1 The Structure of the Smartphone*

The smartphone is the inseparable companion of our lives. It is not unusual to see people on the street who seem to be talking to themselves. If we look at them more closely, however, we realize that they have a smartphone in their hands and are talking to someone. They are focused on the conversation, closed in their communicative bubble, they do not look where they are going and often end up bumping into us.

Due to this device, there is a dual dislocation of those who use it. Whoever uses it, is physically present, but at the same time they are connected elsewhere. People continue to be part of the everyday world, and within certain limits they cannot refuse this role, but the most important things for them are happening out of this space. That is why so many women and men do not worry about sharing their own personal facts on the telephone, whether it's on a train or in a waiting room, in front of everyone. The telephone interlocutor is the most important thing, not the public.

These situations, however, are only possible because the smartphone is really something that is physically always with us. It is a "palmtop" (PDA), a small computer that fits in the palm of your hand. For many things it has replaced the computer, especially when functioning as an "access door" for many connections. Indeed, the smartphone, is even more engaging than the computer, as the relationships it provides are implemented not only through the senses of sight and touch, but more so by the sense of hearing. The smartphone is in fact, let's not forget, a mobile phone development. The use of our voice, to communicate and to be in relation with others, is therefore a priority.

Let's take a moment to think about this last statement. I have just said something that to a certain point is certainly correct, but that is also misleading, and that requires some clarification to be fully true. Generally speaking the smartphone is used for making phone calls, but nowadays we all use it more often for other purposes. We use it to access Facebook, to post tweets, to send emails, to connect to Instagram, to watch a movie by downloading it from YouTube, to take pictures, to read a book or a newspaper, to surf the Net, to follow the instructions on a map to reach a certain place, to be updated on the weather, to record a conversation, to consult a dictionary, to get a taxi. This and much more is made possible by this device, as well as, of course, communicating through voice (calls) or pictures (video calls). That is why, more than the computer, it is currently the true companion of our lives. That is why referring to "communication" is intended primarily as a "call" (to phone). In the case of the smartphone it is somewhat true, but also partial and misleading (Woyke 2014).

### 2.5.2 *Integration and Convergence*

All of this, as we have seen, is due to the fact that the smartphone, like the computer, can integrate different devices into one single device. But what the smartphone offers is not just an example of technological *integration*. It, moreover, works as a true *convergence* between the various functions that are relevant to some media and their multiple contents. In this case, that is, a single device allows access to different communication services, to connect them, even to mix them together. Using the same device, for example, we can take a picture, upload it to WhatsApp, send it, reply to comments, archive this chat. And maybe, with a special program, we can transform the picture, we just took and sent, into something else.

However, this is a process far beyond the development and the ability in the use of certain media. We are not only subject to certain technologies, but we determine their success depending on our needs and the use we make of them. Consequently, we are not dealing with only the concept of "convergence" that is applied in the multimedia digital field (Negroponte 1996). Since technological devices are able to open true environments in which we can live, this notion has a meaning that extends from the purely technological dimension to a more specific cultural field.

When considering things from this point of view, one can speak of "convergence culture" (Jenkins 2006). A "convergence culture" is one in which the same contents are shifted from one medium to another, they are decontextualized and re-contextualized, and in the end they may eventually be contaminated by each other. In this way the distinction between "high" and "low", "elite" or "mass", "local" or "global" culture is diminished. What matters is reciprocal interaction and the permeability of different perspectives.

I have to emphasize that this process occurs not only by virtue of the internal logic of technological development, but as a result of a change of mentality affecting the subjects of communication. The latter, even in the forms of participation made possible by technologies, come to form a sort of "collective intelligence" (Lévy 1999), putting together and transforming different cultural products. We are working this new culture, interacting with the opportunities offered by new devices.

### 2.5.3 *Impossible Immediacy: Apps, Selfies, the Perception of Space and Time*

A very interesting feature of our relationship with technology emerges from this point in time. There is almost a tendency for mutual reflection between what we do and the way machines operate. It has a specular characteristic. But before analysing it, I have to point out another aspect of the operating structure of the smartphone, which strongly affects our behaviour. The smartphone can displace whoever is using it, it can be an example of technological integration, and it can contribute to the creation of cultural convergence just because it uses certain mobile applications (apps).

Applications are for the smartphone the same as what programmes are for the computer. These are application softwares that are used especially in the case of mobile devices. That's precisely why they are simplified software to the maximum, in order to be able to run quickly and require little memory.

It is not the case here to make a distinction between apps that are downloaded and used exclusively on one's own device, rather than those that link us to an available Web service, or to insist on the difference between free and paid apps. What matters is how the structure of the smartphone, how it is made and works in its hardware and apps, ends up changing our mind-set and limiting the space of our choices. There are two points I would like to highlight, and that are linked together. Firstly, the loss of immediacy and secondly the change in our perception of space and time.

Like any device we're dealing with, the smartphone is also a channel of communication. As such it acts as an interface between the various subjects of communication. Here we can find a mediation that is never neutral. As we have certainly seen, very often it allows us to enhance our communication activities, coordination and development. It also opens up the area of interest in which such communication can be realized and contributes to its maintenance. Like any technological device, the smartphone, when working as an interface, it is developed to act, to some extent, autonomously. It turns out that we are interacting with it, therefore it is not a simple tool that we have full control of, nor a machine we are passively effected by. The first consequence of this interaction is the progressive shrinking, if not the complete elimination, of our ability to have immediate, direct relationships with the world and with other human beings.

Every communication device is, of course, a filter between us and the world, even if we often do not realize it and although it seems that, for example, thanks to the TV, we are offered access to "live real life events". But the smartphone performs this feature in a really significant way. First of all, because it is always with us, almost as if it were our prosthesis. As a result, it constantly provides us with a range of services, offering us an orientation of the world. This orientation is not only something real, as in the case of Google Maps, but it also represents something symbolic. It guides us in our lives. Thanks to its structure and functions, the smartphone allows us to see the world as a meaningful place, and it gives us the opportunity to live in other environments different from our own, giving us the chance to operate in both the world we live in and in the virtual environments offered to us by technology.

The price to pay for these opportunities is precisely the loss of immediacy in our relationship with things. There is also the doubt that, with the absence of this immediate relationship, everything we are involved in, mediated by the media, is constructed, artificial and false. It seems then, that the only true, real, authentic relationship can only be with ourselves.

That is why we are increasingly urged to turn to ourselves, to lock ourselves up and to mirror ourselves in our identity. The only sure thing for us is who we are and the image of ourselves. Only what we are of our own image, we can be immediately certain. Our own representation becomes a source of security for us. However, paradoxically, it is also provided by a communicative interface. And so in this time and age, thanks to one of the features of the smartphone, selfies are multiplying.

The term "selfie" was coined in 2004 by a young Flickr user (a photo sharing platform). Today, the self-timer trend and its Web diffusion is extremely widespread. Today there are apps (such as Meitu) devoted to editing and photo retouching of our image, a sort of make-up service to which everyone has access.

It's not just about unleashing ones narcissism. It is not only the attempt to establish a fixed personal image of the personal identity that changes over time, and which nowadays is increasingly uncertain and broken. This phenomenon, which is also spreading not only playfully as in the case of facial recognition programmes, can also be understood as an attempt to maintain, through personal self-representation, at least what remains of that immediacy which the technological age seems to have lost. But it is, of course, a desperate attempt, as a photograph, in fact, never coincides with the original.

Related to this, as a further consequence of the invasive presence in our relationships of a portable communicative interface such as the smartphone, is also the redefinition of the way we normally perceive space and time. What matters now is no longer who is calling us, as this is already written on the display, but to know *where* our interlocutor is (Ferraris 2006). Just as it is important knowing where we are if we want to use certain apps. This function is always automatically guaranteed by the device, unless we disable it.

The smartphone is located at the intersection between these different places. It connects them and mediates them. But it also does something more. It allows us to experience the overlapping, if not the coincidence, of different spaces: the space in which we are physically and the dimensions in which we too live by being connected to them. Therefore, localization is united with delocalization. We are here in one place, but at the same time we are also elsewhere.

I wrote: "at the same time". The mediation that a smartphone puts into operation must actually be realized in the shortest possible time. Connections need to be always faster and faster. Speed is the characteristic of the technological world and the relationships—i.e. the political ones—that develop in it (Virilio 2006). We live in the era of impatience. We can't stand waiting. Everything has to happen "in real time".

Real time is the instant in which all the contacts concerning me are concentrated together at the same time. Real time is the unification of infinite connections at one point, in one node. Real time is the point without dimension where there is a concurrence of each previous process in just one moment.

We perceive this in our use of the smartphone. However, this perception is only partially true. Not only because this concentration of all our connections at the same instant is quickly reinserted within an extended and articulated temporal dimension. Nodes, in fact, are always nodes of a network. But, mainly because as we have already seen this promptness, this immediacy, is provided by a medium, a device that allows us to communicate but that at the same time works as a filter.

Both the overlapping of spaces in which we can live simultaneously in real or virtual ways, both the concurrence of different relationships at the same time, are in fact experiences that only a technological device can activate. Only by means of an interface, we can experience promptness. Pure and simple promptness thus reveals itself as an illusion. Or, at least, it is an illusion that is right for us, which distinguishes our way of perceiving things, which hides all the mediation processes a device makes, even to overcome space-time barriers.

### *2.5.4 How to Live in the World with a Smartphone*

The smartphone is a device that intervenes both to make our relationships possible and to filter them. It enhances our capabilities and at the same time limits them. All this entails a profound change of our way of living in this world. It requires an ethical reflection.

There are two aspects that should be considered. They can be discussed separately, even if they are linked to each other. On the one hand, there are choices to consider as a result of the change in mentality due to the adoption of a certain technological device. On the other hand, it is necessary to consider how the use of this same device should be regulated in various contexts where it can be used, especially in public.

Human beings have always been able to carry out more activities simultaneously. Interaction with multitasking Information Technology (IT) systems, that are able to run multiple programmes at the same time, has further expanded this capability. At the same time, however, this situation requires that among the various processes that can be carried out there must be an order and that they are arranged according to a precise hierarchy of value and priority. Otherwise, there can be a strong sense of disorientation.

We have seen that, in the case of the use of a smartphone, we put into operation both an experience of localization and delocalization and, as far as those who are connected with us, they are drawn closer regardless of their actual physical and temporal distance. From an ethical point of view, however, the problem is not just that. There is not only the need to manage being in multiple locations at one time or to meet our interlocutors in "real time". The question is rather related to the fact that, in a smartphone-driven context, elsewhere is more attractive than here and now, and other people's time prevails over our own.

As a result, what is near ends up being less important than what is at a much greater or lesser distance. Our attention is absorbed more by what is far away rather than by what surrounds us. That's why, for example, we are chatting on Facebook even when we are in the restaurant with our loved one. We prefer to send our friends in real time the photo of what we are eating, rather than talking with the person we have invited to dinner.

All of this is the result of that loss of immediacy. I mentioned earlier. It is not just the recognition, more or less implicit, of the inability to safeguard it when we communicate with our technological devices. It is my consciousness that an immediate, close, concrete relationship has less value than that relationship that is made possible by the mediation of these devices.

If, however, as we have seen, the search for immediacy at all costs is impossible, because each of our communicative relationships always needs a medium or at least one channel, this does not mean that this situation does not have to be governed. It may be by giving value also to what is offered to us in proximity, even in mediated forms. It can be deciding whether, depending on the situation, it has more value than what is presented to us, perhaps in a public context, or what we are connected to remotely. Think again those who, speaking on the phone aloud in a public space, do not care to reveal his personal affairs to others.

It is not simply a question of the etiquette in the use of technological devices, although, of course, a number of prescriptions in this regard linked to good education standards can certainly favour less conflicting inter-personal relations. However, more in general it regards being able to interact with technological devices not only in terms of their operation and procedures, but also and above all with regards to the meaning of the behaviours they promote and the orientation of the world they offer. In short, instead of blindly accepting values transmitted by these devices through the use we make of them, it would be better to put them under critical scrutiny and to interact with them on an ethical basis, by even just turning them off.

## 2.6 Robots, Communication and Ethics

### *2.6.1 Communication and Robots*

Even after reading the pages above we are still unable to put our smartphones aside. We are too used to having them with us. However, every so often it can happen that while we are using it the programme crashes. The smartphone is blocked. That really makes us angry. Smartphones, like any other technological device, can adapt to our needs only within certain limits. In reality, most of the time we are the ones that have to adapt to its characteristics.

In this case, a programme is not working. Maybe we are the ones that don't know how to use it properly, we just might have to delete it and install it again. But before doing that let's make a last try. We ask our voice assistant. We activate it, give certain orders, make our requests and receive some feedback. Maybe the procedure wasn't quite right so we end up swearing and cursing someone. The voice assistant patiently interacts even in this case, inviting us to remain calm.

Technological devices communicate. Not only are they used in communicating, broadening our communication possibilities, unfolding new environments where, as we will see better in the next chapter, our communicative capacity discovers other scenarios. Technological devices also communicate. I would almost be tempted to say that they communicate "directly first-hand".

A movie such as *Her*, which tells the story of a man, Theodore Twombly, who falls in love with the voice of his voice assistant Samantha, while interacting with this programme, or better yet with "her", is the perfect example to help underline how communication between human beings and machines, as in this case, take on the form of a dialogue. A dialogue is a communicative process where various interlocutors can exchange news, information, and content that they understand. In this particular case, the dialogue is between a human being and a machine. Here the dialogue is created by the programme of a machine. And it seems that, from a human point of view, the communicative relationship is satisfactorily fulfilled. In a survey conducted by the US advertising agency J. Walther Thompson in April 2017, 37% of respondents said they were so infatuated by the various Cortana, Alexa or Siri (names given to the voices of various virtual assistants) that they desired or wished they were real.

Let's try and understand why this happens. We will attempt to specify how and within which limits an automated system can "communicate" for real. The assumption of this discourse, however, is more general than that concerning the autonomy of the machine and its ability to make "decisions" so that it can actually interact with humans. Only by clarifying this aspect can we face the problem of machine ethics, how this ethical dimension can affect the communication of both machines and human beings and the concrete problems that this entails. The question, in other words, is related to the relationship—the possible "dialogue"—between two ways of communicating: artificial communication and human communication. Before we address this subject, however, we have to clearly understand which machines we are talking about and what and who these robots capable of communicating are.

### *2.6.2 Anthropomorphic Robots*

When thinking of a robot, the first thing you imagine is a device which usually has the semblance of an animal or a person, with a system and programmes that make it able to move around, unlike a computer on a desk or on your lap, and completed with something like a face. What else would you expect? This is how they are depicted in science fiction books, comics, movies. In fact, the term today has various meanings and is used in many ways. It indicates a mechanism initially designed to carry out various tasks that the human being is unable to do or that are too dangerous. In this sense, the robot is primarily used for industrial, military and rescue purposes in special conditions (Mackinnon 2016).

But this attention to the external form is just one aspect to be taken into account. In order to perform its functions, for example in contexts where high precision or high data processing speed is required, the robot must be equipped with specific programmes. These are programmes that not only analyse and search data in a methodical and automated way, but they are able to process the responses provided by the external sensors of which the robot is equipped and tailored to the jobs it is assigned to. There is, then, an interaction with the environment in which the automated system operates and it has the ability to achieve its goal by following different procedures depending on the various situations.

Taking this into account, the anthropomorphic appearance of the robot is not only the result of something coming from a novel, but is justified for a number of reasons.

The robot has been created to match the human being in its activities and therefore, to fulfil its purpose, it must have some anthropomorphic characteristics (e.g. the ability to grasp objects using something that functions as a hand). Soon, however, it has changed from being a *side by side* system, to an *accompanying* system. The robot was built not only to help and perfect the human being in certain actions (such as surgical operations), but to interact with him or her as a part of the same environment in which the robot works and, perhaps, to assist them in some of their needs (this is the case of the care giver robot or the robot puppy). For this reason the machine must have a "face". The reference to the results (2017) of the FACE project (Facial Automation for Conveying Emotions) may be interesting as it refers to a robot which presents emotional information through facial expressions to study the human–robot empathic link (see www.faceteam.it).

All this has contributed to reinforcing the idea that the robot cannot only support and accompany, but even replace the human being in some activities, by doing it in a better way. And this has caused a number of conflicting reactions. On the one hand, there has been a psychological rejection of human beings towards robots, which is also the basis of those resentful fears that characterize their relationships with them. On the other hand, there is a kind of attraction to these entities, which has produced a dynamic of true reflection between humans and robots: a mirroring, where not only the robots are built to look like humans, assuming anthropomorphic appearances, but in which, conversely, human beings model themselves on robots.

To clarify the first aspect, it is useful to refer to Mori Masahiro's research, known as the "uncanny valley" theory. It demonstrates how the sense of familiarity that we can experience with an anthropomorphic robot grows to the point where its resemblance to humans is enhanced to a point that it does not cause in us an emotional rejection. This is signalled by a sharp curve, known as the "uncanny valley", a curve that represents, in a hypothetical graph, humans attitude to such artificial entities (Mori 1970). This means that the robot has to be recognizable as such, when interacting with us without causing any discomfort, it must look more like a robot without being mistaken for one of us. Perhaps that is why the replicants in the movie *Blade Runner* (1982), directed by Ridley Scott, are hunted down.

In the second case, a different dynamic emerges. It involves a process of reciprocal mirroring between the human sphere and a mechanical operation. More specifically, this reflection occurs in both directions with the use of a mirror, as Lewis Carroll's Alice experiences, for example, when she goes through the mirror in which her image is reflected (thus transforming a fairy-tale world within the effective context of its action). In the image in the mirror, in fact, not only do I recognize myself and contemplate, but in it I can also actively project the best aspects of myself. This results in an exchange of roles between the subject in the mirror and his image, by virtue of which one is alternately a model and to be copied for the behaviours of the other (Fabris 2016).

If in the first case too much resemblance provokes distrust and rejection, in the second case the possibility of seeing oneself as the robot, and vice versa, brings with it a sense of confidence and, sometimes, of exaltation. We are those who, to some extent, can create something made to our "image and likeness" by removing this prerogative to God and biblical tradition (although, in the present state of experimentation, it is more like a Golem than a living being. On the theme of the Golem in cybernetics, make reference to Wiener 1964).

All of this certainly exalts our creative and operational capabilities, it strengthens our actions and our being. On the other hand, however, the direction of mirroring is soon overturned. The model is no longer represented by us, but by the machine which is more perfect and functional in various situations compared to us. We are subject to mistakes, and therefore can never be like a machine. Humans attempt to transform themselves from humans into androids or to standardize people's behaviour to the effectiveness of certain standard procedures. The theories of trans-humanism and post-humanism express this tendency (Ranisch and Sorgner 2014).

In this framework, it is not surprising if an important role is played by communication as well. This occurs at multiple levels. First of all, in our tendency to transfer human characteristics to artificial entities, we are increasingly forced to use words and concepts, that refer to the activities of humans, for these artificial entities to function. At the base of this trend there is certainly a psychological reason. From Fritz Heider and Mary-Ann Simmel's famous experiment (Heider and Simmel 1944), the attitude of humans to attributing anthropomorphic properties to moving objects is well-known, and the interpretation of this movement as an action and this action as being intentional. It is not surprising that the same words are used to indicate both human processes and machine procedures. And yet, we must always keep in mind that the expansion of vocabulary used by humans regarding robots has a metaphorical value. That is why, every time I apply human terminology to artificial entities in this chapter, I care to put these terms in quotation marks.

On the other hand, the application of human categories to artificial contexts seems to find confirmation and support, not only for metaphorical but also literal use of that vocabulary, just as we realize that the machines themselves are able to "communicate". Or, at least, that there are programmes that allow a communicative interaction between machines and humans. The problem is trying to figure out how and within what limits this happens. The problem is to clarify what "communication" means to a robot.

There are several aspects to consider regarding this concept. One must first understand whether such an attribution of communicative capacity to the artificial system is the result of a self-projection on others made by the human beings (as in the case of the attraction to Siri's voice), or if there is a kind of autonomy that really allows the robot, with certain programmes, to communicate appropriately. The meaning of the term "communication" in the case of the robot has to be deepened, resuming the difference between the transmission of data and the opening of a communicative space. It is necessary to check whether the latter aspect of the machine is capable of guaranteeing it can happen, or whether it is, in this case, a task which is only a human being's responsibility and which only they can attribute to the machines. Finally, it is necessary to clarify not only if it is possible that human beings and machines can interact communicatively, but always under the control of human beings, and if they fail to control this, two machines are actually able to communicate with each other, perhaps by constructing their very own code.

In order to deepen these issues, however, first and foremost it is necessary to analyse another aspect. If we will understand how and within what limits robots can communicate, we must make clear whether and to what extent they can be effective partners of such activity, for example in a dialogue. And to decide this, it is necessary to analyse the true assumption of all the issues we are facing: the theme of robot autonomy at current stage of its development.

### *2.6.3 Autonomy and Communication*

For a robot to be considered as something autonomous it needs to be able to communicate and make moral choices (Bekey 2005). The fact that a robot is remotely controlled by a human being, either directly or through a program, is certainly part of the development phase of these machines, in which they are a kind of mediator in cases where human intervention is either dangerous or inaccurate or impossible to realize. However, for a long time this model of relationships—in which the robot must only respond to human intervention, directly or indirectly—has been supported by another paradigm, facilitated by the elaboration of programs by which the robot itself is programmed to interact with its environment and to "learn" from its own mistakes. As is in the case of drones, cars without drivers, and robots that play football in specific matches.

It therefore emerges that this kind of device can accumulate and use a series of information in a form that is the same as what is for human beings the development of an experience. Consequently there are some specific problems that begin to be addressed regarding this. They concern, for example, the possibility that a robot may be legally "responsible" for the consequences of its operation and that it may also be punishable (according to the bill recently submitted by Mady Delvaux to the European Parliament); the idea that a robot can have rights and be endowed with a kind of "electronic personality"; the hypothesis that a robot is a moral subject and can even "learn" to make moral choices as a result of our "education" (according to Regina Rini's proposal: Rini 2017).

From these technological developments, to which the tendency towards reciprocal man–machine mirroring and the identification of their procedures with human behaviours, combined with the imprecision of the commonly used language, derives the conviction that such artificial agents are "autonomous". But specifically what kind of autonomy does this refer to? I have already mentioned the concept of devices that are programmed "to learn" by changing their actions depending on how a certain situation occurs. The famous case of AlphaGo, the programme that was developed by Google to play this ancient Chinese game and which in 2016 beat the reigning champion Lee Sedol 4–1, is certainly the best known example of this capability which characterizes an "artificial intelligence" (AI).

In general, however, the situation for robots is more complex than what it may seem at first. When at work, it performs a network of actions, feedback loops and interactions, which are only partly dependent on its functioning. Each of its actions is oriented and governed by a set of criteria and principles on the basis of which it is realized and involves various levels of responsibility. Here below I can only point them out schematically.

There are above all general principles of reference from which designers, developers and programmers regulate their work and, more generally, their own lives, and which affect the choices that lead to the creation of a certain form of artificial entity. Let's analyse, for example, the case of a pacifist engineer. There are other criteria that motivate people to design, develop and programme a particular machine. These criteria take into account the range of possibility and limits of the technological development of a given era. They are bound to the very structure of the robot and the range of possibility of its action. Furthermore, they are the principles that make the interaction programmes of this artificial agent with its environment and with other beings, artificial or not. Each one of these beings can act in different ways and on the basis of different principles.

In this context talking about the "autonomy" of a machine assumes a definite meaning. We could say that the machine, in our case the robot, is certainly able to *regulate* its own processes, but it is not able to *self-regulate*, or to give to itself norms of conduct. This is the specific meaning of its "self-determination".

In other words, a machine is not able to "choose" the criteria and principles with which it relates to the environment, other machines, or humans, and if necessary to change them. It can only adopt them. In other words, it can follow the criteria and principles on which it was built or programmed. It may also change its way of working as a result of certain scenarios that in general may be pre-determined. But, at least in its present state of development, it is not able to intervene on the basic principles that its construction and operation depends on, as well as how it interacts with its environment. This is the specific form of ethical self-reliance that does not, at this time, occur.

Autonomy, in short, is about how the machine activates its programmes, calculates possible scenarios and responds to them. It is something that relates to the machine's procedures and the ways in which it can be followed. It is therefore a "relative autonomy" on the criteria that the robot has been built, in the specific context in which it operates, within the framework of anticipated options, on the ways in which it responds to a precise environmental stress which have been prefigured, and the rules that, in certain cases, can be followed to achieve the goals set.

I will return to this aspect in-depth, further analysing the ethical vocation of the robot. Now, however, one must see how this sense of relative autonomy, in the case of the machine, affects its ability to communicate, and above all to communicate in a way that makes it an actual interlocutor for the human being. With respect to the issues raised at the end of the previous paragraph, it is to be said that at present the robot is able to communicate in the meaning of data processing and transmission. This distinguishes it from the more extensive, communicative modes that are relevant to human beings.

At the same time, however, the robot has also been developed to process and acquire an interactive ability to make statements, responses, and human emotions. This allows him to express, in such forms of communicative interaction, a kind of correspondence, a capacity to respond "in tone", which can be exchanged for "empathy". This is all the more so because the human being is projecting on the artificial agent, according to the mechanisms we have seen, a certain "sensitivity", or even the ability to "suffer".

From this point of view, most of the communication done, in the perspective of the creation of a communicative space in which it is placed for all human and non-human interlocutors, is carried out by human beings. In other words, the difference between human and non-human is something that is managed by the human being itself. We can do this because we are able to imagine, and by doing so, interpreting different situations of our own, and therefore communicating within them, giving a voice to non-human subjects as well.

However, such imagination is different from the forecast of scenarios that can accomplish an automated system. The imagination of the human being anticipates without calculating, it leaves space to willingly rely on the unexpected. An artificial agent, when communicating, can exercise its role only by probabilistic calculation of alternatives, in order to control what will happen in future scenarios. That is why a robot can never be religious, in the sense of at least the three Biblical monotheism: it lacks the possibility to rely on Ultimate Reality, that is, the option of faith.

All of this has its consequences and its confirmation, for example, within a dialogue. Is it possible to talk with an artificial communication system? Of course it is. And it can also be something productive, to the extent that a real exchange of information can occur. But when searching for a deeper interaction, a true "fusion of horizons" (Gadamer 2004: 304) that addresses the same principles and criteria underlying the positions of the subjects involved in the dialogue, then this interaction can only be managed by a human being. Only when the interaction turns from cooperative, as in this case, to competitive, then the power of calculation and anticipation of the artificial system will probably have the upper hand as was in the case of AlphaGo. But for this kind of match there have to be strict rules and an artificial battleground, on which the unexpected turns in life are only simulated.

In relation to this, there are also clear limits where, no longer, only a human being and a robot can communicate with each other, but also two artificial agents can do the same. They can communicate within a context of predefined rules, but which are not made by them. They are able to develop, simplify and perfect their own rules within a given context. This has been demonstrated recently in an experiment conducted by Facebook programmers, in which two programmes written to imitate our conversation, at one point began to interact with each other using the English language in a different way than usual.

### *2.6.4 Ethics and Robot Communication*

So, robots can communicate. Their communication, however, is carried out according to exact specifications. It is the transmission of data, it takes place according to pre-established programmes, it is able to adapt to the interlocutor and it can "learn" from various communicative situations. Within these limits a dialogue between a human being and an automatic communication system is possible. At least in a specific sense of the word "dialogue".

In the case of the robot this ability of interaction, even communicative, is made possible by some sort of autonomy, that is the "relative" autonomy that characterizes it. But this condition of autonomy is also one that makes it possible to exercise actions that can be recognized and qualified as "ethics". It is the presence of this feature, in fact, that changes the context outlined so far. Up until now we have looked at devices such as computers and smartphones that, by virtue of their features, interact with us, change our behaviours, affect our choices, and that's why they have an impact that must be ethically or deontologically managed. But in the case of artificial communication systems, for example the robots I referred to before, it goes beyond this and there is also the possibility of an autonomous communicative action. This requires that there is the possibility that ethics will not only affect our behaviours, but also the actions that are relevant to such machines.

I have already mentioned this scenario in the previous chapters, clarifying that the term "Ethics of Information and Communication Technologies" is meant not only for the case of reflection on human behaviours made possible by such technologies (objective genitive) but also about the act that is accomplished by certain devices through which we communicate, and that interact with our way of communicating and which in turn communicate (subjective genitive). These devices are characterized by a degree of autonomy that we need to start dealing with properly.

How and within what limits can this happen? Let's talk about the ethical vocation of robots interrupted in the previous paragraph. The robot is called to follow the procedure, not to choose to follow it. That is why, more than just ethics on what is "good" or "bad", or rather than the realization of what is "good" or "evil", in the case of such devices, we must rather refer to what is "right" or "wrong", "correct" or "incorrect".

And yet, even if you are careful about what lexicon you use, it is not enough. There are moral conflicts that are also posed in the case of robot work: not only in the context of those "behaviours" that a procedure has the task of regulating, but also between the same procedure and what it does not foresee. Or, unless a further procedure has been established to govern different scenarios or possible unexpected scenarios, conflicts may arise between alternative procedures, to the extent that they refer to different moral orders. For example, should a non-driver car steer in order to avoid pedestrians or not, if this entails a risk for other vehicles or for their own passengers? So far, one of the ways in which you try to answer this and other similar questions is the one that refers to the choices of the majority, but of the majority of humans (see moralmachine.mit.edu).

Here arises another aspect of that complexity, of that true superabundance in the principles of orientation that characterizes the scope of human ethics rather than that of purely procedural management of behaviours. Human beings live their ethical vocation while maintaining themselves on two levels. On the one hand, applying the rules, on the other hand questioning them and deliberating perhaps to choose different sets of norms. Machines, in order to achieve the same result, need to refer to different procedures that allow them to control the options produced by other scenarios, to calculate what can happen in them, and thus to avoid that arbitrary decisions are made.

Isaac Asimov, a famous science fiction author, was the first person that looked for a reconciliation, specifically in reference to robots, among the demands inherent in the task of following a procedure and the need to handle moral conflicts between different background options. As is well known, the author of *I, Robot* introduced in the novel *Runaround* three fundamental laws regulating the "behaviour" of these autonomous systems (Asimov 2004). On the basis of these laws, the robots were ordered to protect humans, then to obey their orders and finally to preserve themselves as robots. In the event of conflict between these rules, the priority order of their application was to be that displayed.

This is, as you can see, meta-norms: rule-related to the use of rules. They are, therefore, general principles from which the concrete "behaviour" of the machines, regulated by specific procedures, are in fact justified. These are, however, rules that are imposed on robots by humans as general principles aimed at guiding the actions of such machines as a whole. As a frame-rule, in short, they provide a background in which to support the adoption of certain procedures, especially in cases where conflicts arise between them. But in actual fact these rules fulfill their task by following once again the strategy that is relevant to each procedure. And they are useless in the event that a machine is told to choose between different value horizons. Although it is not excluded that in the near future, as some authors argue (Linn et al. 2009; Wallach and Allen 2009) one can speak of "moral machines" in a sense of the term "morality" more like the one referring to humans.

Therefore, the underlying issue is the possibility, in the case of machines and their ethics, to take their actions beyond a purely procedural horizon. Ethics, in fact, is not merely a series of procedures. And this applies to both general ethics and communication ethics.

## References

Ahlstrom-Vij K (2013) Epistemic paternalism: a defence. Palgrave Macmillan, London

Ahlstrom-Vij K (2017) L'outsourcing cognitivo pone un problema epistemico? Iride 80(1):107–123. https://doi.org/10.1414/86524

Anders G (2002) Die Antiquiertheit des Menschen, 1, Über die Seele im Zeitalter der zweiten industriellen Revolution. Beck, München

Apel K-O (1998) Towards a transformation of philosophy. Marquette University Press, Milwaukee

Aristotle (1924) Metaphysics. Oxford University Press, Oxford

Asimov I (2004) I robot. Bantam Dell, New York

Bekey GA (2005) Autonomous robots. Bradford Publishing, Denver

Benjamin W (2012) The work of art in the age of mechanical reproduction. Prism Key Press, New York

Briggs A, Burke P (2010) A social history of the media: from Gutenberg to the internet. Polity Press, Cambridge
Canetti E (1984) Crowds and power. Ferrar, Straus and Giroux, New York
Diebold J (1983) Automation: the advent of automated factory. American Management Association, New York
Drushel BE, German K (eds) (2011) Ethics of emerging media. The Continuum International Publishing Group, New York
Eugeni R (2015) La condizione post-mediale. La Scuola, Brescia
Fabris A (2016) Philosophy, images, and the mirror of machines. In: Paič Z, Purgar K (eds) Theorizing images. Cambridge Scholars Publishing, Newcastle upon Tyne
Ferraris M (2006) Dove sei? Ontologia del telefonino. Bompiani, Milano
Floridi L (ed) (2010) The Cambridge handbook of information and computer ethics. Cambridge University Press, Cambridge
Floridi L (2013) The ethics of information. Oxford University Press, Oxford
Gadamer H-G (2004) Truth and method. Bloomsbury Academic, London
Gomery D, Pafort-Overduin C (2011) Movie history. A survey. Routledge, London
Heider F, Simmel M (1944) An Experimental study of apparent behavior. Am J Psychol 57:243–259. https://doi.org/10.2307/1416950
Himanen P (2010) The hacker ethic and the spirit of the information age. Random House, London
Jenkins H (2006) Convergence culture: where old and new media collide. New York University Press, New York
Johnson DG (2009) Computer ethics. Pearson, London, New York
Lévy P (1999) Collective intelligence: mankind's emerging world in cyberspace. Perseus Books, Cambridge, Massachusetts
Linn P, Abney K, Beckey GA (2009) robot ethics: the ethical and social implications of robotics. The M.I.T Press, Cambridge
Mackinnon P (2016) Robotics: everything you Need to know about robotics from beginner to expert. CreateSpace Independent Publishing Platform
Manetti G, Fabris A (2011) Comunicazione. La Scuola, Brescia
Migga Kizza J (2013) Ethical and Social issues in the information age. Springer, London, Heidelberg, New York, Dordrecht
Mori M (1970) The uncanny valley. Energy 7(4):33–35
Negroponte N (1996) Being digital. Vintage Books, New York
Quinn M (2012) Ethics for the information age. Addison Wesley-Pearson, London, New York
Raffoul F (2010) The origins of responsibility. Indiana University Press, Bloomington and Indianapolis
Ranisch R, Sorgner SL (eds) (2014) Post-and transhumanism: an introduction. Lang, Frankfurt a.M
Reynolds GW (2013) Ethics in information technology. Southwestern Publishing Group, Nashville
Rini R (2017) Raising good robots. www.aeon.co, published on 18th April
Riva G (2014) Nativi digitali. Crescere e apprendere nel mondo dei nuovi media. il Mulino, Bologna
Sanders AF, Brinkman B (2013) Ethics in a computing culture. Delmar Learning-Cengage Learning, London
Segall K (2012) Insanely simple: the obsession that drives apple's success. Penguin Random House, London
Segall K (2016) Think simple: how smart leaders defeat complexity. Penguin Random House, London
Simons GL (1988) Is god a programmer? Religion in the computer age. Prentice Hall, Upper Saddle River
Stamatellos G (2007) Computer ethics: a global perspective. Jones & Bartlett Publishers, Sudbury
Tavani HT (2012) Ethics and technology: controversies, questions and strategies for ethical computing. Wiley, Hoboken

Virilio P (2006) Speed and politics. Semiotext(e), Los Angeles
Wallach W, Allen C (2009) Moral machines. Teaching robots right from wrong. Oxford University Press, Oxford, New York
Wiener N (1964) God and Golem, Inc. A comment on certain points where cybernetics impinges on religion. The M.I.T. Press, Cambridge
Wiener N (2013) Cybernetics: or control and communication in the animal and in the machine. Martino Fine Books, Eastford
Woyke E (2014) The smartphone: anatomy of an industry. The New Press, New York

# Chapter 3
# The Ethics of Communication Environments

**Abstract** This chapter analyses the idea of communication as not being simply just something that we do, but as something that we live. Communication is understood as an environment in which we move. This is a "virtual" environment that needs to be added to the "natural" ones with which human beings have commonly interacted throughout history. Communication technologies, including the devices analysed in the previous chapter, are able to open, maintain, and develop this environment. Even in this case it is true to say that we are talking about multiple environments. They are, as I mentioned above, virtual environments. More than simulations of reality through a machine, they are found in a widespread and daily manner on the Internet, taking into consideration the various phases in which they are involved. After clarifying how communication is to be understood today as a living environment, this chapter will deepen the concept of "virtual" in its various meanings and provide a reconstruction of the history of the Internet and its various developments. In particular, the Internet of Netsurfers, the Internet of Social Networks and the Internet of Things will be analysed. In all of these cases, the customs and habits (*ethos*) promoted by the Network will be examined in depth and will highlight the problems that are related to them, and the criteria and principles of behaviour that allow people to move in these environments in a good way.

**Keywords** Virtuality · Ethics · Internet · Netsurfers · Social Networks
Internet of Things

## 3.1 Communication as an Environment

Communication today is not only something we do, but something we live. It is not simply an activity that is accomplished by human beings, and to some extent also by artificial entities, but it is also the environment in which we move and interact with. This is the situation that characterizes our era and whereby technological developments have made this possible. From this point on, we must understand, in every aspect, the term "communication".



A. Fabris, *Ethics of Information and Communication Technologies*,
SpringerBriefs on Ethical and Legal Issues in Biomedicine and Technology,
https://doi.org/10.1007/978-3-319-75511-3_3

In the first chapter, we introduced the idea of "communication" as "putting together", "sharing", "creating and maintaining a common space". This concept has been elaborated since the ancient world. We saw that it corresponds to the etymology of the Latin term "communication" (connected to the word "*communis*"). Furthermore, in the mid-twentieth century, it was elaborated in another conception by Shannon and Weaver, whereby "communicating" meant transmitting data and information from a sender to a receiver. This idea of communication was functional to the design of a new discipline, cybernetics, and soon was accepted by the sciences of language, allowing it to interpret every inter-human relationship as a form of transmission. This also came to be because certain devices that transmitted data and information, first in an analog mode and then in a digital mode, allowed us to realize in the second half of the twentieth century a series of connections that were continuous, capillary, and that developed on a global level.

In the previous chapter we analysed all of this and we also saw how these devices work—in particular, the computer, the smartphone, and the robot which is capable of "communicating"—and we discovered that they don't just transmit data and information in an increasingly massive and fast way, but they open up an access to further communications which exist only thanks to these devices and which are powered by them. The computer, the smartphone, and the robot are, as we have seen, real "Keymasters" that allow people to enter into a global communication network, within which communication is created (by spoken or written word, through photographs or videos, or by symbols or sounds).

In this way a true transformation of the very concept of "communication" occurs. It no longer indicates the interaction between human beings, in order to create a common space. It does not even mean sending and transmitting data—between machines and humans, among human beings, from one machine to another—and awaiting feedback. Communication is what happens in a particular context of relationships, precisely because this context is made possible and constantly fuelled by the act of communicating.

All this, I repeat, is produced by the powerful and widespread transmission of data and information caused by the development of communication devices. They are the communication technologies which we interact and integrate with on a daily basis in our everyday lives, and which affect our daily environment and create more environments for our activities. In other words, it is the systematic spread of data transmission and information that once again causes communication to bring about the opening of a shared space. This time, however, it is shared globally. Moreover, it involves communicative agents. They are virtually connected to each other from everywhere. They can be, moreover, both human and non-human.

There is a word we have already encountered and that expresses this transformation of communication into environment: it is the word "infosphere". The infosphere is the complexity of information entities in which we are immersed and of their mutual interactions. The term had been used already in the early 1970s, but with reference to offline media. Luciano Floridi, as we have seen, considered the infosphere as the data and information environment in which we constantly live and interact with, both offline and online, the same as what the biosphere is for all living beings

(Floridi 2014, Chap. 2). However, if the term “infosphere” indicates, we may say, the context of all communicative contexts (online and offline worlds), in turn the word “cyberspace” defines, in a more restricted way, the sphere that only includes online communications. It is precisely on cyberspace that I will dwell in this chapter.

So far, I have dealt with the communication environment and I have spoken about “infosphere”. It would seem, as we have said, that the environment in which we move by communicating, and by communicating we make present, is generally only one. That is not true. This, in fact, is another characteristic of our age: that there is a *plurality* of communication environments. There are not only offline and online contexts, but within these dimensions there are also those contexts that are open and fed, transformed and manipulated by the various communication media.

This is something completely new, compared to the past. Today we can live—in parallel, alternatively, or by superimposing everyone of them—within many different communication environments. Therefore, there is a need to move within them and among them in a conscious and competent way. In the past, this was not perceived as a problem, at least it did not have to be dealt with in such an urgent way. Fantasy worlds found in a book, for example, were mostly tied to the text, accessible only to those who knew how to read, and limited by the time needed for reading it, and yet distinct from everyday life.

It is no longer so easy to delimit this situation today. Today, as we have seen, we cannot easily break away from those devices that continuously introduce us into new communication environments. We cannot do this because the very power of the device lies in its ability to keep us attracted to it. And on the other hand, thanks to the ever-increasing performance of these devices, what we find in such environments is not only almost real, but is now part of our perception of reality.

As we well know, the environments, opened up to us by various devices and that are fed, transformed and manipulated by them, are numerous and growing in number. We can therefore easily pass from one to the other. We are even motivated to mistake one for the other. These environments are all familiar to us, they are now part of our everyday lives. That’s why we risk overlapping them. That’s why sometimes we confuse the online world with the offline world.

All this raises a series of problems. They are primarily caused by the need to link, and in a correct and good relationship, the various environments in which we can live through our enhanced communicative capacity. These are then issues related to the need to orient our actions within each of these communication environments. Ultimately, we also assume responsibility for what, as the effect of a network action that only partly depends on us, escapes our control.

Ethics, referring to the era of information and communication technologies, has the task of addressing these issues. The question, I repeat, is how to distinguish these different environments, link them to each other, move from one to the other in a conscious and competent way, and live within each of them in a good manner. The question concerns both the way we deal with such environments and the way we live within them.

But, firstly, why should we have to worry about all of this? Why not let everything take its course? Why don't we just simply adapt to what technological developments make possible for us nowadays?

An immediate response to these questions can be given by making reference to a famous movie, or better so, trilogy: *The Matrix* (1999), directed by the Wachowski sisters. As we already know, this trilogy is the story of a world dominated by machines that create the artificial worlds in which people live, in a state similar to sleep but believing they are making real-life human experiences. In this situation there is a possibility for human beings to wake up, to become aware of their state, to deal with it, to discover the reality that is concealed by artificial worlds, to move adequately between these various levels in which their lives flow. This is the ethical possibility that the protagonists of *The Matrix* choose and for which they fight.

Regardless of the fact that the trilogy stakes this situation by making leverage on a well-defined fear—the fear of human beings in the face of technology that can be now fully autonomous and able to derive from these same beings the energy that allows them to function—it outlines in general a condition that we have to face today. It is the opportunity to live in more worlds; it is the danger of confusing them, until they replace the truth with lies. However, *The Matrix* achieves its purpose, well-sighted, in a paradoxical manner. It does not refer to everyday reality, it does not open to it, it can't be proved wrong as it is something completely fiction, but it simply warns against the risks of confusing reality with fiction by using the modules and language of a fantasy story.

In any case, even with this approach, *The Matrix* describes precisely some aspects of the situation in which we live, even if bringing it to the extreme consequences, and the risks that follow. With regard to them, and with regard to a communicative context that has become an environment of life, we must always take two steps. We must first analyse it. And then ask ourselves how to act within it. Above all, we need to clarify what this means, here and now, to act well and to justify that kind of action.

That is why in this chapter I will try to analyse the relationship between communication and the technological environment by first deepening the notion, that more than any other, allows us to define this environment: the notion of "virtuality". I will try to show the potentialities and limitations of what this notion designates. And I will try to show how we can act ethically both in relation to virtual environments and within them.

From here I will conduct a in-depth analysis of the Internet, since it is the most attractive and widespread virtual environment that exists today. I will consider the various forms of the Internet as they have developed in their recent history and that are still connected to one another: the Netsurfers Internet, the Social Network Internet (or Web 2.0, according to the expression introduced in 2004 by O'Reilly Media), and the so-called Internet of Things. In the following paragraphs, I will investigate some ethical implications in reference to them. I will make it clear, in various cases, the ethics *of* Internet and the ethics *in* Internet, by discussing the problems that the presence of these new environments entails and the ways in which it is good for us to move within them.

## 3.2 Ethics and Virtuality

### *3.2.1 What Does "Virtuality" Mean?*

First of all, what does the concept of "virtuality" mean? How can we deepen the meaning of this word beyond its everyday use? This is a complex notion that has a precise etymology, articulated history and, consequently, a stratification of meanings (see, above all, Ventimiglia 2004; Diodato 2005; Fabris 2007; Crowston et al. 2007: about the difference between Virtuality and Virtualization; Vitali Rosati 2012).

The adjective "virtual" derives from the Latin "*virtualis*", which in turn refers to the noun "*virtus*". "*Virtus*" literally means "virtue". But this represents the first ambiguity. "*Virtus*" is not just a moral concept, it does not only mean virtue that helps to make a human being a good being. It also indicates a characteristic, a capacity that is proper to something and which is related to its essence: as when one is told that a particular plant has beneficial virtues.

This "virtue", this essence capable of acting upon something, is certainly present in something, but it is not always active. It must be put in the condition to exist. In other words, it is something that is there, but that is not yet fully realized. Think of, for example, in the case of Christian doctrine, the way in which the world, before being created, is *in mente Dei* (in God's mind). That is, the perfections of all things that pre-exist, in a perfect way, before the act of creation. This means that in God there has always been the power to make real the effects, the existing things, that pre-exist perfectly in the effective cause (that is God). They are not only a simple possibility. More precisely, they pre-exist rather in a virtual way. This is the meaning in which Thomas Aquinas uses the term "virtually" (St. Thomas Aquinas 1981: 21; see ST, I, q. 4 a. 2).

All these multiple meanings—the moral one, the one that refers to an essence that has not yet been realized, and the one in which this essence is able to activate itself—are present even within the twentieth century and are repurposed in the term "virtual" as it is used in the technical language and in the common speech of today. I can give three examples of this.

The concept is primarily used by Henry Bergson, who refers to the opposed idea of something that is "possible" to be understood as a mere anticipation of the reality that is to come, to point out on the contrary what has certain potential implementation lines (some of which will be made real and others that won't), based on the unpredictable creativity of human beings (Bergson 2010, Chap. 1). It is then used by Deleuze, who develops to the extreme consequences Bergson's thesis of virtual as an ever-new creative force to actualise the individual (Deleuze and Parnet 2012: 112–122). Then, finally, this term assumes a more precise, not philosophical meaning, as a result of certain technological developments. It indicates that "reality" in which we can "immerge ourselves" by simply using a helmet, gloves and headphones with specific sensors, although this reality is not perceived by our senses as we usually use them, but it is the result of an artificial simulation made possible by technology (Linowes 2015). The "virtual reality", moreover, is related to an "augmented reality", in which a computer generated imagery (generated i.e. by smartphones, tablets, gaming systems, or used in some museum exhibits) is superimposed over our perception of the real world (Peddie 2017).

From these recent uses of the term we can reconfirm the idea that, in general, the word "virtual" has to do with certain essential characteristics of something. However, these are features that are not always perceptible by human beings and open up to further possibilities, that can be realized or achieved at another ontological level. If, on the other hand, these characteristics are perceptible, they are on a level different from that of the common experience that each of us can have in a concrete way. It is technology that gives you access to this additional level.

Keeping in mind the etymology of the term and its uses, and trying to better organise the various meanings this notion has taken in the history of thought, we can give now the term "virtual" an overall definition. "Virtual", thus, can indicate both what is simply possible, and as such contrasts with the reality we experience on a daily basis, and both with what potentially exists, and has not yet being made real. In both cases, reference to many classical authors in the history of philosophy from Aristotle to Leibniz can be made to better understand these concepts of "possibility" and "reality", "potentiality" and "actuality" (Vitali Rosati 2012). It is to be said, however, that with regard to virtual, the sphere of possibility and that of potentiality are much wider, they are constituted by many more objects than the sphere of everyday experience.

However, referring to these concepts is not enough. It is not enough, to fully understand the word "virtual", to refer to the above mentioned, and even expanded, terms of "possible" and "potential", or to contrast it with the concepts of "real" (an opposition however, as we have already seen, that is inadequate for Bergson) or "actual" (as Lévy does in the wake of Bergson and Deleuze: Lévy 1998). In addition to this, "virtual" also expresses a positive attitude: it expresses an active power of something, a force that is in itself capable of moving into action.

What is defined as virtual, not only has a certain capacity, a certain *virtus* that characterizes it, but in addition it has the power to bring it to life. It does not need anything else to do so, as it is simply part of its being. It is understood, therefore, that virtual indicates an infinite capacity for self-realization. One understands why, according to Thomas Aquinas, it is a word that can be used to characterize God and his perfect power of creating what he has virtually in mind.

From this point of view, the concept of "virtual" performs almost as a synthesis of the notions of "possible", "potential" and "power" as they were defined in the history of thought. And a similar tendency of unification is equally expressed by this term when referring to commonly opposed concepts, such as "possibility" versus "reality", and "potentiality" versus "actuality". Such oppositions, for example, which are based on the Aristotelian tradition, no longer have any reason to exist: to the extent that what is possible in a virtual environment has already been realized and what seems to be only potential has the power to become real. That is why the expression "virtual reality", which in ordinary language would look like an oxymoron, is in fact not at all.

All of this has been made possible thanks to technological developments and, more so, the ability to process devices capable of opening new environments. This is what we have seen, specifically, with the transformation of communication from an act to an environment of possible relationships. These are always seen as possible relationships, which can always be activated, but which are, however, still largely in place, even when we do not realize them concretely. It is in fact a matter of virtual relationships.

The condition of virtuality, that is relevant to communication environments made possible by technological developments, is therefore a condition that has to do with a relational dimension. It effects our relationships that are already in place and it creates new ones. This also happens because, as we have seen, the concept of "virtual" is in itself a concept that connects various notions together, such as "possible", "potential", "power", "actuality", and "reality".

These are all put in a very special relationship. They are put in relation among themselves as to unify and identify themselves. They are put in a relationship where the differences among these concepts tend to disappear. All this, however, creates a number of problems. These are issues that need to be tackled from an ethical point of view.

### 3.2.2 *Two Ethical Problems*

Above all, here are two ethical issues that emerge in relation to the concept of "virtual" previously analysed, at least two of the implications of this concept that make us live in a specific way, for the most part uncritically, "virtual reality". This is first of all the idea that virtual is immediately considered something virtuous, and secondly the tendency to make no difference between the various aspects, among the different levels, and the multiple opportunities that in the virtual world are linked to each other.

The first idea is tied to the common conviction, that everything that comes from technological progress is intrinsically *good*. For this reason, everything that makes this progress possible is usually pursued, no questions asked. This is simply because when an opportunity presents itself it's always a good idea to give it a go. We have already come across this attitude when talking about computer developments.

In the case of the concept of "virtual", however, if we take this perspective, it is not difficult to retrieve the reference to "virtue" that was implied in the Latin term "*virtualis*". Virtual reality, in this way, seems to be intrinsically and immediately good, and this is precisely why it is virtuous to completely take advantage of what it proposes. It is seen as being something good because it has an infinite expansion, it can incorporate every other imaginable reality, it is able, thanks to the abundance of solutions included in it, to answer all sorts of problems. That is why virtual reality seems to be able to offer human beings that consolation and salvation from the evils of the world that in the past were provided by religious beliefs. Further confirmation is found, if we consider the various ways in which death is dealt with on the Web and how there are procedures to guarantee a perpetual memory online of the deceased, making one "immortal" (Moreman and Lewis 2014; Ziccardi 2017).

In other words, whoever enters into a virtual environment does not want to miss out on anything. They always have it on their mind and live it every way, those who sit in front of the computer, give up every concrete relationship that they have: those who are called "*Hikikomori*", a term the Japanese use to call these people who sit in front of the computer all day and lose the sense of reality leaving all concrete relationships aside (Tamaki 2013). Virtual reality, in fact, is less demanding, it is always available through the filter of one device or other. So living in it may seem preferable: like someone in a role-playing game.

Furthermore, if actions taken in a virtual context are less demanding because they are accomplished within a reality where everything seems possible, they also seem to have less responsibility than those in the offline world. It always seems like you can go back in time, and that what is done over time can be reversed, but this is not at all true. People seem to forget that even what is done in the virtual world has an impact on our everyday life, and that it is irreversible.

Those who forget are usually people who confuse one level of reality with another, meaning that one doesn't know how to distinguish offline reality from virtual reality. For him or her everything is the same. Everything is interchangeable. Everything can be exchanged one for the other. *Indifference*: this is the second fundamental idea that comes from imposing a virtual dimension. This represents yet another problem we must learn to deal with.

We have seen that the concept of "virtual" expresses a condition in which the concepts of what is "possible", "potential", "powerful", "real", "actual" are almost always confused one with the other. I would like to repeat that in the notion of "virtuality", there is the tendency to blend and confuse all these aspects. In addition, if the absorbing capacity that is relevant to this concept is true, even between the world of a sensorial offline experience and the technological environments that we live in, there is the risk that the difference is not perceived.

So, the task that we are now facing is how to deal with this indifference. First of all we have to realize this trend exists. Then we must reject the attempt of those who find it useless in the technological age to distinguish between real and virtual, and who claim that the only reality there is, is in fact a "virtual reality". If that were truly the case, then ethical consequences would be disruptive. We would find ourselves again in front of a "one-dimensional man", to use a famous expression of Herbert Marcuse (Marcuse 1991): even though this dimension, today, would be the one that virtually includes them all.

By contrast, it would be best to deal with such indifference. To this end, it is necessary to restore the differences within that dimension that tends to cancel them. It can be done in two ways, which are the ones in which human beings try to pull themselves away from the attraction of the virtual world.

The first concept is tied to the assumption of a fundamental difference between what is happening daily offline and what we can experience online. It's about not losing the ability to reflect and make decisions in *reference to* what is virtual. The second way is to deal with this tendency of indifference, which the concept of "virtuality" expresses and that virtual reality produces, and to find within the virtual environment various levels of interaction, different from each other, that cannot be put all on the same plane. It is about acquiring the ability to orientate oneself *within* the virtual world. Both of these attitudes, as we shall see, can enable us to develop and practice ethics of virtual relationships.

### *3.2.3 "In" and "Out of" the Virtual Experience*

If the virtual dimension is an all-engaging, attractive, indifferent and all-absorbing dimension, the question that arises from an ethical point of view is that, in that dimension there is no room for exercising the ability to decide. Or rather, there is only one initial decision that can be taken more or less consciously: to be embedded, to adapt to the opportunities offered by what is virtual. It may, of course, be a comfortable and, perhaps, fulfilling situation. But after we adopt it, we also give up making other decisions. We have delegated someone else—may be the "Big Brother" of Orwell's book *1984*, the "matrix" of the Wachowski sisters' movie *The Matrix*—to schedule what I have to do and what I have to think.

It is better, however, to regain our capacity to be moral subjects. We can do so only by regaining the possibility of deciding. Also in relation to the same situation in which we live; also with regard to the virtual reality from which we can be absorbed.

We can only acquire this possibility if we leave this environment. Or rather, if we live within this virtual environment, well aware that it is not the only one we can live in. There is virtual reality, of course. But it is not the only form of reality.

What does it mean to leave what is virtual in order to retrieve the possibility of making a decision? What does the possibility of assuming an "external" prospect of the virtual world imply? It makes it possible for us to confront ourselves with something virtual from an ethical point of view. But there are two ways to do this, thanks to this ability to live both "out" of the virtual environment and "inside" it. We can reflect on our attitudes towards this environment, taking into account its characteristics, and we can search for the criteria and principles that can guide our actions within it so that it can be considered good. In other words, we can develop ethics *of* the virtual world or develop ethics *in* the virtual world.

These two approaches need an in-depth analysis. To do so, it is necessary to now analyse the environment in which virtual has found its most widespread and best expression. I am referring to the Network, more so to the Internet.

## 3.3 The Internet and Its Phases

Nowadays, the Internet is the best and most widespread example of a communication environment offered by technology. Up until today it has gone through three different phases, which, although still present in our daily use, need to be analysed separately.

This is what we can call *the Internet of Netsurfers*, *the Internet of Social Networks* (or Web 2.0), *the Internet of Things.*

Previously, I already mentioned the logic of hypertext and the World Wide Web. As we already know, the Internet was born for military needs (with the launch of the ARPANET project in 1960) and since 1969 it has had a further application by keeping researchers in touch with various universities. It was given this name in 1982, after the TCP/IP protocol had been defined (i.e. the transmission control protocol and the control protocol from one network to another), and it spread widely following the development of the World Wide Web (a system for sharing information in hypertext, developed by Tim Berners-Lee). Since 1991 it has been increasingly used for commercial purposes, and since 1995 it has become popular thanks to the introduction of the Explorer browser icon on the desktop of personal computers with Microsoft programmes. This is the development phase that led to the globalization of the Netsurfer Internet, that is, what we can call the "traditional" or "first" (1.0) Internet now: an environment consisting of infinitely linked nodes (sites) that we can visit, one after another (through the link system) driven by our needs or curiosity. It's a kind of ocean on which you can "surf", it's an inexhaustible menu to taste little by little. But—wishing to continue with these metaphors—is also a sea that at the surface it is accessible to everyone, although there is a deeper part: the so-called "Deep Web" (Bartlett 2015).

In fact, in this architecture of the Internet, the contents are already present, predisposed by those who build the sites. Considering this architecture always from the point of view of users, it offers services, information, news that can be accessed, and which are nevertheless preliminarily put on the Network and constantly updated. In any case, even if this update does not take place, the various sites remain available, just like the updated ones, and they are listed by the search engines. The "Deep Web", on the other hand, is the name that indicates the set of information resources that cannot be drawn through normal search engines. They are therefore inaccessible through the usual channels.

In any case, at this stage of the Internet, the use of data is largely passive, as it is the traditional mass media. The activity required by netsurfing is the one that allows you to switch from one site to another, to compare the various information and to look for new ones. The problems that emerge here are above all two: finding what one needs and then putting order to all this vast material available. Further on we shall see how this is done.

The second phase of the Internet is that dominated by Social Networks. As always in the history of communication, something is added and does not immediately substitute the previous communication system available. Here the content is presented as it is provided by the various users. Everyone, thanks to a simplification of the programmes used, can upload data directly to the Web and edit it (such as files, images, videos). This data, in turn, is shared, exchanged, commented by people connected to the Network: they become a social asset (Prell 2012).

At this stage, this is what information and communication technologies have to offer as environments in which we move: now not only just information or predefined services, although they are constantly growing and available for research, but the possibility of an expression of the users themselves, by sharing contents, and creating a communicative participation among those who exchange them. It seems that the ancient concept of "communication" as the sharing of a common space, is being re-proposed. But some problems have come up: that, for example, of delimiting this space, since for its proper use it cannot coincide with the entire Web; and then, how can we establish and govern relations within the various communities. I will go back to these and other problems later.

The last significant phase in the history of the Internet for now is what concerns the so-called "Internet of Things". In this case, it is no longer human beings that are connected to each other through the Network, but they are a series of devices that, on the Net, perform some functions and with which humans interact. Think of the developments of domotics. It is the discipline that studies and creates the devices that are connected to each other, capable of producing a "smart home": a home, that is capable of improving the environments we live in every day (Greengard 2015).

We've already seen how robots that can communicate with each other and with humans are made. With the development of technology, more and more the conception of a space inhabited not only by natural entities but also by artificial structures is spreading. Both entities tend to get confused when it comes to integration. The problem here is how to handle this relationship correctly. The problem, more specifically, relates to how people take on the responsibility of this situation and deal with it: the issue of its control and the transformation, which is demanded, of the concept of "responsibility".

In the following paragraphs I will address these various aspects of Internet development. The aim of this is to elaborate, specifically, Internet Ethics. Internet Ethics can be elaborated following the same approach that we introduced and justified in the case of our most general interaction with virtual environments. In regards to this, I had distinguished between ethics *of* the virtual world and ethics *in* the virtual world, so now I will develop on the Ethics *of* the Internet and Ethics *in* the Internet. To do so, I will analyse the three cases I have already mentioned: the Internet of Netsurfers, the Internet of Social Networks and the Internet of Things.

But what do I precisely mean, when using these formulas? Ethics *of* the Internet is the reflection on issues related to the impact of the Internet on society, the world we live in, our way of thinking, regardless of whether we actually relate to the Network professionally or not. It has to do with the structure of the Network and the consequences that various aspects of the Internet have on our lives (Cavalier 2005; Bouchon 2005). In fact, even if we are not programmers, webmasters, operators who work on the Web or we are not even ordinary users of the Network—although in the case of younger generations this is a rare case—we are still part of a world that the Internet is changing.

Ethics *in* the Internet, however, refers to the set of behaviours, considered good and right, which are taken on by those who work or, more generally, act within the Network. This is the reflection that seeks to answer the question on how to regulate the various activities that are made possible by the Internet. It can be done again, either through a deontological approach or with an ethical approach.

In one case and the other, the assumption that is implicitly taken on—the assumption without which no ethics is possible—is that the person that has to do with the Internet, both offline and online, is still free, meaning he or she may decide to connect or not, and when connected to the Network they can behave in a good manner or in a bad one. The Internet is a new environment with which we interact and from which we can assess the implications, but it is not a necessary destiny from which the human being cannot escape. So the way in which interact with the Internet environment and make precise choices within it depends on us and calls into play the our sense of responsibility.

## 3.4 Ethics and the Internet

### *3.4.1 Issues on the Ethics of the Internet*

The Ethics *of* the Internet, I repeat, is about how we can evaluate and judge "from outside" the various aspects that are relevant to the structure of the Internet, regardless of whether or not we operate in this environment. Above all, there are two concepts I want to analyse by adopting this perspective. They are ethical issues linked to what is generally called the "digital divide" and related to the non-neutrality of the results proposed by various search engines.

More specifically, the first phenomenon that I intend to consider is, from a geopolitical perspective, referred to as "digital divide", whereas, if seen from a social point of view, it is called the "cultural divide". Indeed, the Internet greatly increases access to information and to the exchange of knowledge, but it is equally true that these opportunities are not guaranteed to everyone in the same way. Indeed, in the geography of the Internet, there is a considerable worldwide imbalance between places that have long been connected to the Network and places that are not at all, or that they are not adequately connected. Just as there is a similar imbalance between the areas directly crossed by the telecommunication infrastructures and those that have to refer to the infrastructure of others.

This is what the "digital divide" is. It is not a static phenomenon, but it is something that progressively increases the gap between the various parts of the world with regard to access to specific opportunities. However, the expression does not only indicate technological inequality. In fact, digital divide affects all those possibilities of innovation, knowledge development and economic growth that today depend on effective Internet access. Its consequences, therefore, have a much wider impact on a cultural plan.

In this way, there is a division even within one society, when, as is often the case, not all groups or individuals belonging to it possess the cultural instruments, the mental opening and the know-how to take advantage of the opportunities offered by the Internet. This is what is called the "cultural divide". The expression indicates the imbalances caused by generational differences, mentality, and know-how.

In this case, the problem is not only the access to the opportunities offered by technologies, considered in a global dimension, but rather the imbalance within the same society. It is due to the different cultural capacity of its members—young and old, educated and uneducated, rich and poor—to conform to the ever-new technological developments, and the constant need to be updated that they require. It is evident, however, that the emergence of such cultural inequalities within a society also affects the global inequalities that are caused by the digital divide (Walsham 2001).

Of course, it is true that the concept of "digital divide", if dealt with in all its aspects, is a "unclear" concept (Stahl in Floridi 2010: 107), somewhat ambiguous and hard to define. But it is equally true that, in the same way as the concept of "cultural divide", it is possible to bring out a situation of actual inequality that is caused and maintained by the structure of the Internet. In other words, this is a problem of inequality in the distribution of those assets and of those life chances that should be guaranteed to each human being.

For this reason both digital divide and cultural divide are a matter of primary importance for the ethics of Internet. This is primarily a matter of justice. Justice must be understood here as fairness, that is, to guarantee to all equal access to the same opportunities (Rawls 1999). Ethics, then, is used not only to identify the criteria that allow such access, but also to legitimise and justify it. From this point of view, the way in which ethics addresses these issues is the basis of any kind of action on a social level and any initiative at a political one: both national and international.

The second phenomenon that I want to analyse from an ethical point of view refers to the apparent neutrality of search engine results. To do so we need to be able to break away from the Internet and consider its dynamics from "outside". I have already said that, to "surf" quickly and effectively in the "sea" of the Internet, we cannot rely solely on our capabilities. The infinite menu that the Network offers us requires that an orientation policy be provided to make the most of its opportunities. In other words, we must be able to quickly find exactly what we need. This is what search engines are used for.

A search engine is an automatic system that analyses a set of data and presents an indexed list of content available that can satisfy our request. Thanks to this process we can get the information we need. Such information, however, is provided in the form of an index, that is, a list of a number of sites we can link to. And these indexed sites are arranged in a certain order.

This is precisely the problem: the order of the results we are offered is not decided by us but by the system. And this order is not based on our needs, or on the reasons that prompt us to search for something on the Web. These needs and reasons may change from time to time, and even if we take them into consideration they will still end up changing the order of the results. The system, however, proceeds in its classification automatically, based on statistical-mathematical formulas (the famous algorithms I have already mentioned) that are able to submit the required information promptly in a given order.

A number of issues emerge from this and need to be taken into account when using search engines. Regardless of the apparent objectivity with which they propose their results, their research is not at all neutral and their results cannot be considered objective. They depend more on how the research system is programmed. There is also to be said that, in order to provide its results, it is programmed in a unique and fixed way, regardless of what may be the reason that led us to a particular investigation. In other words, it is a rigid system. We have to interact with this characteristic (Bronner 2013).

Usually, in the most popular search engines, the criteria for which the list of sites presented after a certain request made by us is based on the site which has been viewed the most, therefore the most popular site. The value of what is offered as a response, its placement in the ranking we are presented, depends on its popularity, that is, how many Internet users have previously visited that site. Other criteria, such as the competence or reliability of the content provider, are not usually considered: criteria which application does not always produce the same results as that related to its popularity.

There has certainly been a fine-tuning of the research procedures in recent years. To the extent that one or more tags, namely a label that allows you to further identify it on a personal interest basis, is associated with certain information about an object, and research can be developed more accurately. Tags too, however, are mechanically detected by the system. We are thus far from that flexibility and the progressive self-correction that characterise the processes of human inquiry.

There is therefore a definite and partial approach that characterizes the mechanism of search engines. Moreover, this is a partiality that intervenes in an already delimited context. As I said, search engines do not index everything in the Web. There are various resources that are not normally reported by them. This is what, as already mentioned, is called the "Deep Web". Regardless of the relationships that are made possible and in many cases go beyond what is legal, the fact that the Deep Web is overlooked by the indexing is another limit of the search engines.

Usually, however, we disregard this partiality and these limits. On the contrary, we rely on our research, and then we delegate our choices regarding the criteria to be adopted, system procedures, confiding in the objectivity of their results. Most of the time we do it without thinking. Moreover, it is very often the case that among the thousands of results that within a few seconds the search engine proposes us, we limit ourselves to considering only the ones reported in the first pages. We accept from the system, in short, not just the criteria on which the search is made, but also the indication of what, according to these criteria, is more relevant.

To this we can add a last aspect, which intersects with a further element that I will discuss later on, which regards the safeguarding our privacy. Any research that we make is in fact traced and preserved. Based on this we can build a kind of profile of the needs we have manifested. This profile is then used to propose certain offers by letting us try to consolidate our presence on certain sites and promote the purchase of certain products. Our data, in some cases, ends up being marketed. I will come back to that shortly.

What can the Ethics *of* the Internet do about this? Not much, of course, on a practical level, and yet something essential. The Ethics of the Internet has the task of understanding the situation determined by the use of these communication technologies and identifying the fundamentals that govern it. Only from this point can we take back, within certain limits, that possibility of choice which allows us to act in a good way within the Internet and to interact with its structure. Only in this way a good behaviour in our online interactions is not something of a fad. To give indications on this is the task of Ethics *in* Internet.

### 3.4.2 Ethics in the Internet

The Ethics *in* the Internet, as I have said, intends to regulate the behaviours of those who work and act within the Network and define, justify, and promote the wise choices made when using the Web. There are two ways in which this can happen. The first one refers to a deontological approach. The second leads us to a more ethical field.

The deontological approach is what, with regard to behaviours adopted on a Network, refers to a series of rules that are outlined in some regulatory codes. This is especially the case when it is not possible to rely on common sense and the criteria of the immediate agreement between individual utility and collective utility (Bronner 2013), since the former, individual utility, risks taking the upper hand. These codes are of various types. They concern or users of the Network, or those who may be interested in the communication activities of those Networks, if not damaged.

In the first case these are codes that seek or rule out general behaviour, or indicate how to build certain communicative products on the Internet. Generic behaviour codes often take the form of advice or rules of good manners, if not of etiquette. In this case we talk about "netiquette", and in some cases even a kind of "handbook" for the use of the Network is proposed. Codes that instead are intended for giving instructions on how specific multimedia texts must or must not be written are for example the rules governing the writing of an email (Rooksby 2002) or a blog, or the participation in a chat or a Social Network.

The second case, then, is that of codes that, instead of considering the behaviour of Internet users, pay more attention to the interest of the various parties involved in processes of communication: the receiver of a communication, for example, or those who are object of the communication itself. This is the case with codes concerning the use of the Internet by public administrations (Homburg 2008). This is especially the case with codes that take into account the consequences of online communication with regard to minors: both as Netsurfers (and therefore exposed to sites that might disturb them), and as being the subject of incorrect practices that could be done on the Web (paedophile pornography, cyberbullying, etc.). In these cases, besides the introduction of rules to guide the correct use of the Web, concrete monitoring and control initiatives are promoted by the sites themselves or by appropriate organizations.

The management of ethical issues in Internet Communication from the elaboration of concrete codes of conduct leaves, however, as in other cases of deontological prescriptions, some perplexity. We have already seen this. Indeed, the merit of the codes is to clearly identify what is allowed and what is prohibited in the use of those tools that make up the Network environment. But the codes, to be functional and effective, can only punish a verified transgression. And here are two issues.

On the one hand, this solution would require the presence of a governing body that oversees the activity that is carried out within a particular environment: a body recognized by everyone and capable of really sanctioning all transgressions. But the establishment of such an organisation is difficult, and its function cannot be extended to the whole Internet. It can certainly concern the specific use of a platform or access to a particular service—as is the case with certain Social Networks—but only within well-defined limits. In this case, if a transgression is detected, the most serious penalty most times is to be excluded from the service available. However, since the Internet is not something managed and supervised by a single entity, it is currently not possible to refer to a monitoring authority that is globally capable of sanctioning transgressions. Without taking into account the fact that the transgressor, by simply changing his or her identity, one can sign up again to the Network service from which he or she was excluded.

On the other hand, reference to codes seems to solve a number of ethical problems with reference to a setting that refers directly to the law. But because of its approach and its interests, ethics is radically distinct from law. I have already mentioned it in the first chapter: while law establishes rules of conduct within a society, and therefore has to do with justice, ethics applies to all human beings and has to do with what is good. That is why, even in the case of the Internet, legal issues are different from ethical issues (Sullins in Floridi 2010: 116–32; Migga Kizza 2013, Chap. 2). And that is why, even when it is difficult, for the reasons I have said, to respond to the transgressions in using the Internet with effective sanctions, anyone who works on the Net is however questioned on their sense of responsibility: involving and calling one into question individually.

Therefore, to regulate behaviours within the Network, an ethical supplement is required. This is the second aspect that refers directly to the Ethics in the Internet. It concerns those choices we have to make if we want to act accordingly in the Network.

In such a situation, however, we need general criteria of orientation. It must not be extrinsic, but compatible with the very structure of the Network. As we have seen, in fact, the Network is a connection structure that is constantly expanding through new connections. It is an artificial device that, however, also corresponds to the specific structure that is, in general, human. We, too, are in relationship with each other, and express ourselves by promoting always new relationships.

If that is the case, we can derive from all of this an indication of well-defined ethical conduct, which applies not only and not so much to our actions in general, but most of all to our actions on the Internet (Fabris 2015). If the Internet is the environment in which we experience being in an online relationship, the best thing to do is to adopt behaviours that favour these relationships, rather than block them. In fact, relationships that produce and promote other ones are good.

Therefore, we have identified a general criteria that can guide us in dealing with the various ethical dilemmas with which we can come to terms with effectively as Internet users. This is the underlying criteria of Ethics in the Internet. For now, let's be content in referring to it as a general concept. Occasions to give a proper overview and verify their validity will follow shortly. We will deal with this in the specific phase of the Internet that is relevant to Social Networks.

## 3.5 Ethics and Social Networks

### *3.5.1 Problems and Opportunities of Social Networks*

As I previously mentioned, *Social Networks*, as an example of the Internet phase called Web 2.0, are characterized by expressiveness and sociality (Kadushin 2012). They are extremely user-friendly and this allows the user to express their individuality, generate new content, and share it with other users within a particular community. It is therefore a platform through which a user can manage both his or her Social Network and social identity: the one with which he or she uses to contact others. From both of these points of view Social Networks are a blog development (a term derived from the contraction of "weblog"): the Web 2.0 tool by which many people put online personal stories or comment publically on the news, perhaps directly on the newspaper site, and are willing to discuss their comments with other readers.

The most popular Social Networks today (2018), at least in Europe, are Facebook, Instagram, WhatsApp and Twitter. However, they all have very different structures. For example, Facebook, Instagram and, in part, WhatsApp allow a group of users to share various multimedia content without anyone else having access to what these users are sharing. The community that is set up is a community that is usually closed, based on specific interests and composed only of "friends" or "friends of friends", although it can certainly expand. Twitter instead allows the broadcaster to send something to its followers or general messages—the most common—or individual messages. In this case, however, those who receive these messages can respond, but do not get in touch with the other followers of the same issuer. In other words, while in the case of Facebook, Instagram and WhatsApp the communicative relationship is horizontal and reciprocal, in the case of Twitter is more vertical and hierarchical (Fabris 2017).

This is the structure that makes it possible to express and share our identity and experiences through Social Networks. This identity is not only something that is predetermined, in a profile made mostly of a text and an image, but also of what is progressively constructed and confirmed by the materials from one's life-image, videos, comments that are shared from time to time. It is therefore a fluid, fragile identity: constantly reconstructed and confirmed through online relationships.

Taking into account these characteristics of Social Networks some issues emerge that need to be analysed from an ethical point of view (see Kadushin 2012, Chap. 2). It will be this, indeed, the way I intend to elaborate, here, an ethics of Social Networks. I want to concentrate in particular on two situations: the transformation of the idea of "community" they produce and the issue of the treatment of personal identity.

Referring to the first point, regardless of the different structure most common Social Networks have, it is with no doubt that the possibility that these Networks offer in expressing ones opinion and sharing them within a community has led to the widespread idea that each user not only has the undeniable right to express his or her opinion, but is even authorized to manifest it, even if one does not have the competences recognized to do so authoritatively. All one needs is that there is a community in which he or she is placed, and where one can comment or welcome an opinion with a simple "like", or that he or she has "followers". Herc, in other words, emerges a deeper, substantial horizontality than the one which refers to the way in which some Social Networks are structured: it in fact involves being on the same level as all those who have access to the platform.

This is a particular interpretation of the concept of "equality". Here the equality of opportunities, which access to the platform precisely guarantees, is likely to become the homologation of everyone in the community. They participate and have the right to express their opinion to the extent and within the limits of the structure of the platform itself. Not only does the need for recognition of more competence fail, but the very functioning of this structure eliminates any difference between the skills, the preparation, the experience of the users. In short, the possibility that Social Networks offers of expressing views and sharing it makes one forget that an opinion may be more or less valid and that, in any case, it must be argued.

However, without this possibility, opinions and news, and then real and fake news end up being placed on the same level as the different opinions, and then they go viral. If in fact the acknowledgment of the authority of the source of news is lost, if it is sufficient that there is only one opinion on something, whatever it is, then it is no longer important that the information is verified, but that the opinion expressed simply corresponds to what I'm already convinced of. And in fact the spreading of news that takes place according to the logic of Social Networks is that of the so-called "Filter Bubble": the bubble where everyone receives only the information that interests them and confirms their views (Pariser 2011).

The uniformity of Social Networks, the fact that it is enough to be connected, to be empowered, and to one's views validly, the lack of authority and the need to distinguish what is true from what is false, thus transforms, together with the concept of "public opinion", also our idea of community (Byung-Chul 2013; Bronner 2013). And this has a number of very precise consequences also on a political plan. In fact, despite the ability to comment extensively on what is being posted, the reaction of the members of the community is often limited to a like or a dislike. This is certainly the way in which opinions are shared.

But "sharing" is not the same thing as "participating". Here is a point that has a very important consequence on a political plan. Participation is in fact the result of a confrontation of opinions, requiring them to be argued and that, at the end, the best judgment is chosen. It is the way in which decisions within a democratic regime are taken, or should be taken. If this is not the case, if one considers the expression of an immediate preference for or against a given opinion as being the same as a weighted decision, then democracy is certainly weakened.

However, all of this is also the result of a true transformation of identity, which depends on the structure of Social Networks. In this context, as I have said, we present ourselves through our profile, but we also confirm who we are through what we share. We can certainly open up various accounts, we can lie about who we are, we can assume the identity of someone else, but in any case we are forced to a certain degree of consistency in our activity on this or that of the Social Network.

Precisely because it is a social identity, however, two aspects need to be considered carefully. On the one hand, this identity is established and developed only through relationships. On the other hand, for this reason, it is more fragile and requires, in the case of younger users, attention and caution in online interactions, in order not to damage ones identity offline through what happens online. From this perspective it is likely that nowadays certain phenomenon such as the destruction of a person's reputation and cyberbullying arise.

All this relates to the idea that the *self-expression* that Social Networks make possible coincides with a complete and a non-problematic presentation of who we are. The fundamental value, which Social Networks seem to provide, is that of transparency. However, on one hand this transparency is made possible by the overabundance of information we can obtain online, making it difficult for us to orient ourselves and therefore needs to be managed properly. On the other hand, it seems like we are completely giving up our privacy. Faced with this situation, of widespread lack of discretion, some have referred to it as a true "pornification of the society" (Ess 2009).

All of this is certainly the result, as I said before, of a transformation of how personal identity is conceived and practiced within Social Networks. Sharing your personal data doesn't seem to be a problem; very often safeguarding your privacy doesn't seem to be a primary concern. To add to this, Social Networks are referred to as places that promote self-expression: where everything we do, even the most trivial things, are shared and commented. This is a further stage of that "Society of the Spectacle" (Debord 2000) that was already widespread with audio-visual communication. Only that today, thanks to the Network, each one of us can be the protagonist, the director and the producer of our own show. As long as our audience of "friends" don't abandon it.

### *3.5.2 Can Social Networks Be Regulated?*

This situation needs to be regulated. This is possible if once again a connection to either a deontological level or a more ethical ground is made. In both cases one could refer to it as the ethics *in* Social Networks.

With regard to the deontological approach, in this case it assumes a well-defined configuration. It does not concern those general terms that could regulate some of the uses of the Web. Instead, it is about how a particular platform—whether Facebook, Twitter, or anything else—is self-regulating and regulating its use. These are the rules that each user must formally accept when you sign up to access platform services.

This need is generally understandable. We've seen that: for the type of community to whom a Social Network allows access, there is a set of rules that make it possible to define how this community started, how it shaped its own space with respect to other communities, and how it developed on the Web. But soon we learn that, it turns out that these regulations are not totally in favour of the members of the community, who are simply offered the platform for interaction, but primarily it favours the interests of the companies that govern Social Networks. These interests are related to the acquisition of our information and data, and which we freely share while using a platform.

In particular, there are two issues at stake. On the one hand, people's privacy is ignored, and on the other, they themselves give up their ownership of the content that they share. The two issues are different, but connected to each other. Everything uploaded on a Social Network becomes, in fact, virtually of public domain, at least for the community of reference. In this way, I not only share what I do and what I am, but I allow both the platform and its users access to what is mine. In the name of transparency, I cannot only forget about any form of discretion, but also give up my rights to the content.

As I have already mentioned in the previous chapter, the latter case is an example of the tendency to diminish intellectual property that the Internet generally favours. Intellectual property is property in the products of the human intellect. Since the Internet offers new ways of creating, presenting and disseminating intellectual creations, it is very difficult to restore the conditions of an appropriate recognition of the work that has led to these creations, especially from an economic point of view. For some, as we have seen, this is good. Everything on the Net must be accessible to everyone. For others, this is not only an economic problem—that has however caused big companies to change their forms of marketing their products—but above all from a legal and ethical point of view (Migga Kizza 2013, Chap. 5).

In the case of the Social Network this situation is mostly defined by the rules of access to one platform or another. From a legal point of view, this is exemplary, and certainly safeguards the interests of who controls the platform itself. In the case of users, more than once, it can happen that dozens of pages where these rules are established and listed, often using technical language, are not read at all, or at least not read carefully. You scroll the cursor quickly to the end of the pages and click on "I agree". What really matters is accessing as soon as possible the opportunities offered by the Social Network that we are signing up to rather than taking time to read.

This is, of course, a behaviour that is often considered hasty and imprudent. Now, in fact, at least we are aware—even after the issue has been highlighted movies and documentaries, such as *Terms and Conditions may apply* (2014)—of what we are giving up. Often those who act in this way only take half the blame as they are convinced that the set of rules they are subject to, are nevertheless prefigured and cannot be negotiated. So in the end it's either take it or leave it.

Faced with this, two options may be adopted, and which are also present in recent movies or documentaries on the subject. I'm referring to *Disconnect* (2012) and Wener Herzog's video *Lo and Behold* (2016). The first is still a deontological solution and it refers to your right to privacy using the same legal instruments used to regulate a platform. You can't do this by negotiating individually with the Social Network, but it can be done by working with the other users to try to find wider, and more general regulations with other users with whom each Social Network should operate. This is what should guarantee a global authority. There are already measures taken that go in this direction by individual States or, for example, by the European Community (European Commission for Competition). But for the moment we are still far from a definite solution.

There remains, perhaps, another possibility: the assumption of a proper ethical behaviour by individual users. The reference, in this case, is to a category of ancient ethics, the just mentioned category of "prudence". It is about balancing the opportunities that Social Networks guarantee with the risks associated with the absence of privacy and the ownership of the content we put on the Net. It is a matter of finding a balance between these two concepts.

The opportunity is that we are offered to build something new together, using very specific forms of communication. But this is an opportunity that must be exercised with caution: without confusing, as we have seen, the concept of sharing with participating, and on the other hand the idea of putting ourselves on display by using our own forms of expressions. However, we have already defined the ethical criteria that allows us to see how far we can push ourselves in holding these two concepts together. It is the ethical criteria for which, in a social relationship, it is good to do all it takes to positively promote this relationship, not to destroy it. This general criteria can also be applied to the Social Networks field, identifying the limit beyond which a relationship is no longer so and the community, formed by people connected to one another, becomes an undistinguished mass.

To prevent this from happening there is, however, one last thing to keep in mind. It is not a good thing to completely give up your privacy—it is not possible. I'm talking about what our identity is both online and offline. In fact, any form of social relationship exists only between identities that are somewhat different and remain different, even when developing a relationship. If we do not safeguard the spaces in which we can be ourselves and confuse what we really are with how we appear on the Net, then in the end we will have nothing to say: neither inside a Social Network nor outside of it.

## 3.6 Ethics and the Internet of Things

### *3.6.1 Things on the Net*

Collective intelligence (Lévy 1997) is no longer constituted by the relationships of humans through the Network. It is no longer powered by their connections. Today, intelligence, as we have seen, is also "artificial intelligence" (AI). Such intelligence is also exercised through multiple forms of relationships. Today, however, these relationships are no longer merely those that link the action of this or that device with human being's actions but they involve the devices themselves. They can be connected to each other. This is the artificial configuration that collective intelligence assumes today. This is about the *Internet of Things*.

The expression "the Internet of Things" was first used by Kevin Ashton. It indicates the Network of devices other than computers that are connected to the Internet and which, through the Internet, are able to exchange data and information. The "things" mentioned are, as I have said, devices but also systems, and furthermore objects. For example: cameras or traffic lights, home heating systems or freight containers. What matters is that they have a software that allows them to exchange information: among themselves and between them and the Network nodes. Each object, as long as it has this capacity to connect, it can therefore become part of the larger dimension of the Internet of Things.

For this connection to be made possible, so that the various "things" can communicate and "talk" with each other, it is necessary not only that they have a connection software, but also that this connection takes place independently from human intervention. Connecting is therefore the sign of the autonomy of the device on the Network. In addition, in order for this autonomy to be recognized as specific to a particular "thing", this device must also have its "electronic identity". It is an IP (Internet Protocol) address that constitutes the identification label of a device and allows it to be uniquely established that the information sent is transmitted directly from it.

Autonomy and identification, together with the fact that they exercise their "intelligence" through specific connections, are therefore the main characteristics of "things" connected to each other through the Internet. There are many examples already widespread in which all this is accomplished, and many more will come in the future. Today, they relate in particular to the use of energy and transport management. Both cases can be exemplified by referring to existing Network optimization procedures by streamlining them through the connections of these "things". On a wider scale, the example is offered by the so-called "smart cities" (Houbing et al. 2017). At a scale closer to the size of our everyday activity we can refer to the idea of the "smart home", which deals with domotics.

I do not want to analyse in detail these specific areas of application of the Internet of Things. I can only confine myself to mention, for example, smart road technology in the case of smart city and intelligent heating system in the case of a smart home. The first one connects, for example, road sensors, traffic lights and traffic, in order to efficiently govern a city's traffic, i.e. to optimize its flow and reduce overall pollution. The second is that, through sensors that record the changes of temperature of a home and the actual presence of its inhabitants, and who are able to "learn" through these interactions, it is able to achieve real energy savings.

In both cases, the human being is affected by these processes. You can simply choose to subdue to them or try to interact with them. There are therefore some ethical issues that we must now discuss.

### 3.6.2 Some Ethical Issues

We can do this, by keeping in mind the set of ideas expressed until now. We can analyse our relationship with these technologies or by keeping "out" of it, or considering ourselves part of the environment they create. There is, however, an important novelty compared to what we saw earlier when we looked at the Netsurfers Internet and at Social Networks. From the Internet of Things, in fact, in principle we are excluded. In this case it is the "things" that interact with each other. One cannot therefore speak of an ethics *in* the Internet of Things, if "ethics" refers to the criteria and principles that guide human action. One can speak of "ethics" in another sense, which specifically relates to the actions of the devices.

The concrete ethical issues that emerge considering this scenario are notoriously linked to the huge mass of data that is collected by the various devices placed on the Network. It's not just about the data that is needed to reach the goal that is specifically of a certain device connected with others, but also other data that are collected anyhow. This refers to the concept of "big data" (Holmes 2017).

The question then is: what should be done with all of this data? How can it be handled? Furthermore, is it legal to collect and store it? The problem is due to the fact that in almost all cases the consensus for this collection is not required. For example, think of the many surveillance cameras, scattered at different locations, which video us without us knowing. Think of all the tracks we leave when we surf the Internet.

Two more problems can be added to this. The first one has been mentioned several times. If a variety of data is collected through the Internet of Things, and this happens almost always without our consent, all of this puts our privacy at risk. If then there is the possibility to access this stored data and to use it, always without our explicit consent, the question becomes even more complex. Using this data allows us not only to define our profile from the tracks we leave, and are recorded by various devices—as for example with our Network behaviour. In this case, it is the act of "things", their "behaviour" that automatically records the data that concerns us; it is their operation, regardless of the use we make of these devices, that is able to trace our profile. Think of all the information about our private habits that can be derived from the operation of an intelligent heating system.

The way in which these consequences are normally justified is what refers to the overall efficient improvement of the system, but also to the security that comes from this network connection. The basic idea is that greater transparency guarantees greater security. The waiver of privacy, or much of it, is therefore the price to pay to achieve this goal.

However, this is not exactly true. We are, in fact, aware that there is a further aspect that needs to be taken into account. The multiplication of connected devices weakens the security of the system and makes it more susceptible to computer attacks. The more number of devices connected to the Network, not always sufficiently protected, the greater the possibility that the system may be hacked.

But these problems—the problems that relate to the big data management, privacy conservation, and security threats—are just specific, concrete issues. To address them, we can once more refer to deontological solutions. Big data management can be subject to controls and limitations, access to sensitive data is already and can be increasingly safeguarded, a higher level of security can also be guaranteed through an ad hoc regulatory mechanism. All this can be done and is in fact accomplished, with the limits we have already pointed out, through rules and regulations to punish all possible transgressors.

There is, however, a fundamental question that cannot be addressed with a deontological approach. Instead, it must be highlighted and managed in a specifically ethical manner. This is how we can relate, in a correct and good relationship, with the various online and offline environments in which we live today.

So far, we have seen how we live daily with those technological environments that are open to us by various communicative devices. We have seen how we can ethically handle those choices presented to us by these situations. These are environments that overlap with our everyday life, the offline world, expanding our chances of action within a virtual dimension. Now, however, in the case of the Internet of Things, the situation changes decisively. Now we are not moving to a virtual environment. We continue to live in our daily environment, perhaps even widened and increased thanks to interaction with other technology-based environments, but we are excluded from those active relationships that relate only to the "things" and the data they exchange.

We are faced with a new scenario. It happens that the relationship of humans with the Internet of Things is only given before and after it's connected. Before: humans work as designers, programmers, device builders, and networkers. After: to the extent that they may be the end-users of the processed data. In the middle, however, the relationships between the "things" start to develop: relationships, I repeat, from which we are excluded.

But there is also something more. There is the idea that the "smart" environment, the environment in which the "things" are connected to each other, not only overlaps with the environments in which humans move on a daily basis, but it also risks replacing them. In fact, this environment is more rational, structured, more efficient than the world in which things are disconnected and we are, to some extent, the ones who put them in relation with one another. So there is something analogous to what we have seen in the previous chapter, analysing the mirroring relationship between humans and machines. It is now the Network of "things" to form the model of relationships that human beings can implement. It is no longer the single device, with its perfect functioning, but the equally perfect reality of its connections is what attracts us.

In short, from this Network, from the Internet of Things, human beings are largely excluded. Here is the issue to be considered, even from an ethical point of view. If we are excluded from this environment, ethics, in fact, can only partially affect our behaviours, and the criteria and principles that govern them. Therefore, they are called upon only, as I have just said, "before" and "after": in the design and creation, and in the final use. But in the relational intervention of "things" there is no room for human intervention unless it is the intervention of a technician who is called into fix a problem.

Actions taken in this environment are therefore only the act of "things". And even this act, as I have said, is carried out according to the criteria and principles, as is the case for every ethical act. In this case the criteria and principles in question are those of effectiveness and efficiency in data transmission, and are those that aim to ensure the conformity of certain processes to the achievement of a certain objective. This is how a specific procedure is considered "good". But if that is the case, if this is the context that allows us to recognise something as being "good", then it is clear that ethics regulating the actions of these devices is an ethics of utility. The question remains whether the utility should be that of the system, or that of its users.

In any case, if there is no room for human action in the Internet of Things, our ability to control those processes is certainly considered less. But if we lose control we also lose our responsibility. We are no longer able to fully influence the consequences of certain processes. In many cases indeed, in the technological age we are experiencing, we cannot even predict these consequences.

All this raises a last and decisive ethical question. How can we maintain our status of moral beings if we live in environments that are organised independently from our intervention and where we are no longer in full control over the consequences of the actions that are being carried out? This is a question that has often been related to natural events in the past, especially if such events caused unforeseen damage. Now the issue calls into question the artificial agents. We shall discuss it in the Conclusion.

## References


Bartlett J (2015) The dark net: inside the digital underworld. Melville House Publishing, New York

Bergson H (2010) Matter and memory. Digireads Publishing, Overland Park

Bronner G (2013) La démocratie des crédules. PUF, Paris

Bouchon C (2005) Macht das Internet einsam?. Grin Verlag, München

Byung-Chul H (2013) The Burnout society. Stanford University Press, Stanford

Cavalier RJ (ed) (2005) Impact of internet on our moral lives. State University of New York Press, Albany

Crowston K, Sieber S, Wynn E (eds) (2007) Virtuality and virtualization: proceedings of international federation of information processing working groups 8.2 on informations systems and organizations and 9.5 on virtuality and society, July 29–31, 2007, Portland, Oregon, USA. Springer, New York

Debord G (2000) Society of the spectacle. Black & Red, Detroit

Deleuze G, Parnet C (2012) Dialogues II. Continuum, London, New York

Diodato R (2005) Estetica del virtuale. Bruno Mondadori, Milano

Ess Ch (2009) Digital media ethics. Polity Press, Malden

Fabris A (ed) (2007) Etica del virtuale. Vita & Pensiero, Milano

Fabris A (2015) Ethical issues in internet communication. In: Cantoni L, Dobrowski HA (eds) Communication and technology: handbook of communication science. De Gruyter Mouton, Berlin/Boston

Fabris A (2017) Twitter et la philosophie. "Sens Public". Revue Internationale/International Web Journal: www.sens-public.org/article1233.html

Floridi L (2014) The fourth revolution. How the infosphere is reshaping human reality. Oxford University Press, Oxford

Floridi L (ed) (2010) The Cambridge handbook of information and computer ethics. Cambridge University Press, Cambridge
Greengard S (2015) The internet of things. The MIT Press, Cambridge
Holmes DE (2017) Big data: a very short introduction. Oxford University Press, Oxford
Homburg V (2008) Understanding e-government: information systems in public administration. Routledge, London, New York
Houbing S, Ravi S, Tamim S, Jeschke S (2017) Smart cities: foundations, principles, and applications. Wiley, Hoboken
Kadushin Ch (2012) Understanding social networks: theories, concepts, and findings. Oxford University Press, Oxford, New York
Lévy P (1997) Collective intelligence: mankind's emerging world in cyberspace. Plenum Trade, New York
Lévy P (1998) Becoming virtual. Plenum Trade, New York
Linowes J (2015) Unity virtual reality projects. Packt Publishing, Birmingham
Marcuse H (1991) One-dimensional man: studies in the ideology of advanced industrial society. Beacon Press, Boston
Migga Kizza J (2013) Ethical and social issues in the information age. Springer, London, Heidelberg, New York, Dordrecht
Moreman CM, Lewis AD (eds) (2014) Digital death: mortality and beyond in the online age. ABC-CLIO, LLC, Santa Barbara
Pariser E (2011) The filter bubble: how the new personalized web is changing what we read and how we think. Penguin, New York
Peddie J (2017) Augmentad reality: where we will all live. Springer, London, Heidelberg, New York, Dordrecht
Prell Ch (2012) Social network analysis: history, theory and methodology. Sage, Los Angeles, London, New Delhi, Singapore, Washington D.C
Rawls J (1999) A theory of justice. Cambridge, Belknap
Rooksby E (2002) Email and ethics. Routledge, London, New York
St. Thomas Aquinas (1981) Summa Theologica. Translated by the Fathers of the English Dominican Province. Benziger Bros. New York
Tamaki S (2013) Hikikomori: adolescence without end. Minnesota University Press, Minneapolis
Ventimiglia G (2004) Ontologia ed etica del virtuale. Teoria 14(1):119–147
Vitali Rosati M (2012) S'orienter dand le virtuel. Hermann, Paris
Walsham G (2001) Making a world of difference: IT in a global context. Wiley, Chichester
Ziccardi G (2017) Il libro digitale dei morti. Memoria, lutto, eternità e oblio nell'era dei Social Network. UTET, Torino

# Erratum to: Ethics of Information and Communication Technologies

**Erratum to:**
**A. Fabris, *Ethics of Information and Communication Technologies*, SpringerBriefs on Ethical and Legal Issues in Biomedicine and Technology, https://doi.org/10.1007/978-3-319-75511-3**

In the original version of the book, the line "Translation from the English language edition: Ethics of Information and Communication Technologies by Adriano Fabris, © Springer International Publishing AG 2018. All Rights Reserved. © Springer International Publishing AG 2018" was replaced with "Copyright © Springer International Publishing AG 2018. All Rights Reserved." in the Copyright page of the Frontmatter.

---

The updated online version of this book can be found at
https://doi.org/10.1007/978-3-319-75511-3



A. Fabris, *Ethics of Information and Communication Technologies*,
SpringerBriefs on Ethical and Legal Issues in Biomedicine and Technology,
https://doi.org/10.1007/978-3-319-75511-3_4

# Conclusion

A book like this cannot have an ending. Technological developments continue and change the scenarios with which we interact. In some cases, they create environments where devices interact with each other, excluding us. This is the fundamental ethical problem with which we have to deal with. And I will come back to this.

What did this book want to offer? Well, to start with it offered an analysis of the changes that information and communication technologies have produced and are producing on our lives. It has highlighted the main problems that such changes involve. And it has proposed a series of solutions, case by case.

Specifically, it outlined the need for legal regulation of such processes and the development of professional deontology. Generally speaking, it pointed out the criteria that is needed to allow us to recognise what is considered good behaviour. This criteria is what is compatible, and intrinsically connected, with the relational structure of the human being. In order to maintain this structure, in order to reconfirm it, in order to ensure that the human being can continue to be what it was and is, it is necessary to choose the relationships that always promote and produce new relationships. Here is the principle needed to guide us in the different situations we come across as subjects immersed in increasingly communicative environments governed by technology.

Furthermore, we saw how these technologies act in their turn. Devices give access to specific environments. These environments in turn host us, forcing us to confront ourselves with certain situations. In some cases these environments do not need us to work properly. And we are, in fact, having to bear the consequences of what is out of our control.

Regarding this, a last set of questions need to be answered. Answers are needed in order to safeguard an ethical space for the action of humans in the age where even the technologies themselves are able to act. These questions primarily concern the lack of our responsibility for actions that we are not, concretely, doing. Where is our qualification as moral subjects if we have to deal with artificial environments with whom we certainly interact, but without the possibility to have full control

 
A. Fabris, *Ethics of Information and Communication Technologies*,
SpringerBriefs on Ethical and Legal Issues in Biomedicine and Technology,
https://doi.org/10.1007/978-3-319-75511-3

over the devices' actions? Does it still make sense to talk about human "freedom" in such contexts? What is ethics in fact, if there is no free subject that can make certain choices?

To answer these questions—deciding on the legitimacy of the whole course we have followed in this book—we have to make a final reflection. We need to understand, in the case of the human being, what the *responsibility* is and how it is possible to exercise it. The human being is not only responsible for the consequences of an action, nor does one see the responsibility limited to the application of those criteria and of the general principles under which he or she chooses to act. This may still be understood as being part of a procedure, it could be the result of a programme according to a rule or set of rules. Then, in that sense, the responsibility could be attributed to the action of certain technological devices too.

Instead, and above all, the human being is responsible, or rather, freely assumes the responsibility of something more. Not only the relationships it initiates, or the criteria on which these relationships are made, but, primarily, the same relational context, that is, the environment within which it operates. And this can be done by the human being even if that environment does not depend on him or her, even if one does not have full control over it, even if it is already activated by the action of other subjects: natural or artificial that they are. In other words, if the human being recognises this context as the context of his action, as an area in which to interact, also in order to modify it, *one consciously assumes responsibility for what he or she is not responsible.*

This is something that a machine is not able to do yet, as we saw in the second chapter. The machine, though feeding back to the context in which it is operating, cannot question this context as such. It is condemned to reconfirm it, just as it carries out the procedures. The machine is not, however, capable of putting into question the rules used to produce it, and the environment to which the device has access.

Instead, human beings can. It's in our nature to put our same nature in question. Human beings, in fact, can even deny ones nature: as it happens in so many cases in which he or she proves their ability to annihilate themselves or other human beings.

This is what putting our freedom in action means. This involves reconfirming the specificity of being moral subjects. In this emerges the particular way in which we experience our responsibility. Above all, in this there is the need to identify the fundamental difference that, at a time where also devices act, makes it possible for us to ethically interact with information and communication technologies.

MIX
Papier aus verantwortungsvollen Quellen
Paper from responsible sources
FSC® C105338

If you have any concerns about our products,
you can contact us on
**ProductSafety@springernature.com**

In case Publisher is established outside the EU,
the EU authorized representative is:
**Springer Nature Customer Service Center GmbH**
**Europaplatz 3, 69115 Heidelberg, Germany**

Printed by Libri Plureos GmbH
in Hamburg, Germany